THE
FLUTE OF
GOD

Available from Eckankar

The Art of Spiritual Dreaming
Ask the Master, Books 1 and 2
Autobiography of a Modern Prophet
Child in the Wilderness
A Cosmic Sea of Words: The ECKANKAR Lexicon
The Living Word, Books 1 and 2
A Modern Prophet Answers Your Key Questions about Life
Past Lives, Dreams, and Soul Travel
Soul Travelers of the Far Country
The Spiritual Exercises of ECK
The Spiritual Laws of Life
The Temple of ECK
The Wind of Change

The Mahanta Transcripts Series
Journey of Soul, Book 1
How to Find God, Book 2
The Secret Teachings, Book 3
The Golden Heart, Book 4
Cloak of Consciousness, Book 5
Unlocking the Puzzle Box, Book 6
The Eternal Dreamer, Book 7
The Dream Master, Book 8
We Come as Eagles, Book 9
The Drumbeat of Time, Book 10
What Is Spiritual Freedom? Book 11
How the Inner Master Works, Book 12
The Slow Burning Love of God, Book 13
The Secret of Love, Book 14
Our Spiritual Wake-Up Calls, Book 15
How to Survive Spiritually in Our Times, Book 16

Also available from ECKANKAR
ECKANKAR—The Key to Secret Worlds
The Shariyat-Ki-Sugmad, Books One and Two
The Spiritual Notebook
The Tiger's Fang

THE
FLUTE OF
GOD

PAUL TWITCHELL

ECKANKAR
Minneapolis

The Flute of God

Printed in U.S.A.

Twelfth Printing—2004

Cover design by Lois Stanfield

Library of Congress Cataloging-in-Publication Data

Twitchell, Paul, 1908–1971.
    The flute of God / Paul Twitchell.
        p. cm.
    Includes index.
    ISBN 1-57043-032-2 (alk. paper)
    1. Eckankar (Organization)—Doctrines. 2. Spiritual life—
Eckankar (Organization) I. Title.
BP605.E3T8923 1999
299'.93—dc21   98-50432
                                                          CIP

∞ The paper used in this publication meets the minimum requirements of the American National Standard for Information Sciences—Permanence of Paper for Printed Library Materials, ANSI Z39.48-1984.

Contents

Foreword

The teachings of ECK define the nature of Soul. You are Soul, a particle of God sent into this world to gain spiritual experience.

The goal in ECK is spiritual freedom in this lifetime, after which you become a Co-worker with God, both here and in the next world. Karma and reincarnation are primary beliefs.

Key to the ECK teachings is the Mahanta, the Living ECK Master. He has the special ability to act as both the Inner and Outer Master for ECK students. The prophet of Eckankar, he is given respect but is not worshiped. He teaches the sacred name of God, HU. When sung just a few minutes each day, HU will lift you spiritually into the Light and Sound of God—the ECK (Holy Spirit). This easy spiritual exercise and others will purify you. You are then able to accept the full love of God in this lifetime.

Sri Harold Klemp is the Mahanta, the Living ECK Master today. Author of many books, discourses, and articles, he teaches the ins and outs of the spiritual life. His teachings lift people and help them recognize and understand their own experiences in the Light and Sound of God. Many of his talks are available to you on audio- and videocassette.

The Flute of God is a classic work of spiritual literature written by Eckankar's modern-day founder, Paul Twitchell. Within these pages, you'll discover how to build the best possible future and master your spiritual destiny. You'll learn how to listen directly to the guidance of the Holy Spirit.

To find out more about the author and Eckankar, please turn to page 211 in the back of this book.

1

In the Beginning

*F*or one to write his own philosophy of life it might take five minutes or five years. This depends upon the individual and his complexities, gathered during the many incarnations of lives lived in this universe over the years.

The simple man or anyone who has a clear mind will in general say, with a few words, that life goes in certain directions, while the person with many complexities will use words upon words to describe his philosophy of life.

I remember very well when Sudar Singh, the great ECK Master, said, "When someone asked Bertrand Russell what his philosophy of life was, he wrote several volumes of books on the subject."

When Jesus was asked the same question by his disciples, he said, "Thou shalt love the Lord thy God with all thy heart, and with all thy soul, and with all thy strength, and with all thy mind; and thy neighbour as thyself."

The greatest philosophers of the ages stand high above the heads of their fellowmen. They are always looked upon as the redeemers of the human race, who bring the Word of God into this world again and again, especially when mankind is at its lowest spiritual ebb.

But the ECK Masters are far greater than philosophers, for they teach from the heart that man should do for himself. The minister and the priest teach that the organization is greater. No great philosophy has ever come from an organization, but from an individual whose research has been a personal study of God and Its ways.

One must come to the understanding sooner or later that in each period of growth in life there will be a certain teaching designated for a particular area. It is similar to the educational system of this country, whereby the child receives a kindergarten education, later a grade school, then junior high and senior high teaching. If he wishes, college or a university degree can be his, and thence to a master's or doctorate degree.

It is also said to be like that of a parent to a child; when the child grows into the age of maturity there is no further need for dependence upon the parents. Each of us must make our own way through the universe, to see and enter into the knowledge of life itself—in our own way, in the only way we know and understand.

We may have knowledge of the Divine gained from the ECK Master who gives his methods and techniques. If we get the teachings directly from the Supreme Being, by our own individual efforts, through our simplification of personal techniques worked out by our own understanding, we enter the true path in our own way.

During my presence in this physical universe, which has amounted to some eight million years, I came to know so much about life that for centuries I tried to forget. And forget I did!

Knowing that one of the ways to live in this world called the earth planet was to forget who I was—I took no time at all in dropping a curtain over the submind to blot out all records of previous lives in order to be conscious of only one life at a time.

Since the memory of all past events in my life as a sentient being has started to return, hundreds of thousands of little memories creep in day by day that bring up pictures and feelings of yesteryears: Rome, ancient England, Atlantis, the golden age of Greece, India, the planet Clarion, Venus, wars, and love. We can look forward to a greater life than merely reliving former experiences, by becoming a conscious Soul handling the environment, body, life, spirit, or whatever you might call the ECK power, and participating in events of our own creation. Then life becomes the pleasure it should be and could have always been.

We must live life. There is no way out of it regardless of the universe we are in. We cannot die, as spirit, so we must develop in awareness and help others develop until the great Supreme Being, the Life Force known to the Buddhists as the Void, decides that we can become the Co-worker with the Divine.

It is then that we take our places as master craftsmen to help with the controlling of the world of worlds.

I have studied under many ECK Masters, and only they have led me to the highest truth. Like Fubbi Quantz, the ECK saint, who was said to have had nineteen teachers to help him gain his place in the universe, I have also had several, each outstanding, one being Sudar Singh of India.

Each has had a place in my growth toward the spiritual goal; each is equally great in his work for mankind. However, I have felt a closer kinship and friendliness to Sudar Singh, who showed me a lot of the other worlds, during my first year or so under him. Since we have parted he has retained an impartial view toward me and my research. If I quote him in these pages it is because I feel that he was sympathetic, interested in my work, and led me to Rebazar Tarzs.

Many millions of years ago, I came to this planet, knowingly, and with the desire to do my part in furthering the plans of the universal consciousness of God. Everyone understands the plans of God upon this earth, that is, almost everyone.

By this statement, I refer to those people who have full memory of former lives—some do, others do not, and it's best that I direct my attention toward those individuals who do remember.

There are individuals living upon this earth who are centuries old. There is said to be one, a woman, who is supposedly a million years old. Her purpose for living is destruction, and for that reason she passes from one nation to another creating havoc wherever she goes. She is known by many names. In India they call her Kali, the mother goddess, the goddess of destruction.

We cannot deny people longevity if they insist upon it. It is merely a matter of redoing one's relationship with matter, energy, space, and time, and living as one desires.

This does not mean that one is going to live in opposition to the laws of the world made by nature, or whatever you call that mysterious equation.

When one rerelates to the laws of this world knowingly, then he can choose his course of events—but not until then. If he breaks laws unknowingly there will be an increase of trouble for him. He will soon run into difficulty for he does not know how to use the explosive forces he releases. It is sort of a Pandora's box, and confusion and chaos tend to send him spiraling downward into levels of emotional discontent.

I have watched hundreds of people become mixed up and confused in life, get out of touch with life's laws, and die in stolid ignorance. But others lingered on, wondering what was wrong. They did not come to that point which lies just beyond oneself, but remained badly aberrated and could not understand what was wrong with them.

However, there is not much to say about any of this except that one must simply be himself! That and nothing more. The quicker this is accepted, the better developed spiritually one becomes. The individual grows into spiritual serenity by becoming more of one's own self. ― what does this mean

Frankly, very few are able to do anything of themselves. Therefore, they must have a teacher to show them the approach to God. A master is necessary until the disciple is able to walk alone and perhaps become a teacher himself, quite possibly the Master.

This is the cycle of God for man, for man must become as God eventually. There is first the child who seeks, then becomes the man who looks for God everywhere but in the right place. He finds his teacher, becomes the disciple, and finally becomes the Master himself.

This is so very simple. It need not take incarnation after incarnation!

Teaching is not always done in the way one believes. The ECK Master may never utter a word about God. He may use an example. It could be done through a job, a profession, or by means other than oral or written teaching. The Master may not appear to be a teacher to anyone; in fact, those close to him might not even suspect it.

There are a great number of people who love to show what they know. They will invariably talk to you, expressing their opinions and beliefs about God; telling you how much they can help you, even advertising in the press to this effect. Always be skeptical—question everything and everyone. It might be but a dishonest effort on their part to make themselves a living—nothing more. What they know comes a great deal from books with little experience of learning from other teachers, and seldom, if ever, from what God gave them directly. A person who is truly knowledgeable will rarely do a great deal of talking on any subject.

There is no point in resisting these false masters; simply accept them as they are and leave them alone.

The Supreme Consciousness will appear to anyone, provided the individual furnishes the state of consciousness through which it can appear. Therefore, whatever anyone is receiving or lacking in the expression of his consciousness is his own responsibility. It is the result of his own consciousness. Until you can understand this, you can never have true freedom and liberation from this world.

Until you can understand that nothing can happen to you, nothing can ever come to you, or be kept away from you except in accordance with the state of your consciousness, you do not have the key to life.

Life fascinates me. Certain details of life that have to be worked out are strange. Lying on the bed late at night I watch the pattern of shadows weaving about the room. In the presence of familiar night visitors like Sudar Singh and Rebazar Tarzs, the ECK Masters who come often in their Nuri Sarup bodies, or others, some strangers, some friends, I wonder about life.

There are always details that haunt me; perhaps

6

a painting in a gallery in a far-off foreign city, travels across a strange land where I have never been before, the face of a beautiful woman, or maybe a child reaching for a stick of candy.

Each idea is like a bather lingering upon the beach at the water's edge eager to take the plunge and yet fearful of the expected chill. It may be like that of a cathedral standing in the shadows of giant oaks. The main aspect of these and many other illusions is that I am interested in life. These are images that capture my imagination and are real to me, and I try to make them more intimate for others as they meet with my writings.

Do you believe that God cannot do wonders for you? In my life, wonders have happened so often that sometimes I become complacent and think they are commonplace. Then something happens and I am again awakened to what God is doing for me. It is miraculous in this world and other worlds. I do not dispute what God is, and what God does for me in the present, has done in the past and will continue to do for me in the future, throughout eternity.

We do not pray for the Divine to give us something, as individuals. Instead, we ask in a positive manner for that which would benefit all in our receiving. By so doing we are lifting ourselves above the level of self-involving thought and giving greater significance to helping ourselves by doing for others.

What does this do for the individual? Praying in a manner as above keeps the self from forgetting that it is a part of that greater Self we call God. We are gods of course, but gods of our own universe, and gods among other gods. Every man, woman, and child is God! No one can dispute this basic fact of cosmic wisdom! As said before, I am haunted—perhaps haunted by the fact that beyond my concept of God there is something else. The secret of all secrets—and not many know what that might be. I have had an opportunity to catch a glimpse of it, and for that very reason I feel haunted—destined to walk this earth for centuries, among the crowds of the great cities, over the majestic plains, through the jungles, by the rolling seas, and in the mountain heights. Not looking for It, but seeking within myself that which opens the inner sight again to find It in Its wonderful glory!

The closest I can come to It, which I call the Truth, is looking into the heart of a morning glory on some summer morning before the flower has closed its petals to the rays of sunlight. Have you experienced this? My glimpse of the Divine brings with it a strange sound of music with its glories, a marvelous melody sounding like a multitude of flutes. I have called it the Flute of God!

Why is it that so many become upset when hearing the truth? It is because those individuals have not yet developed to the point where they understand that they themselves are God. This statement is so simple that often we overlook who we are—ourselves!

When the ECK Master Gopal Das looked upon his people and said, "I cannot tell you more because you cannot hear the whole of ECK," he was saying that they were so far down the spiral of life they could not grasp his meaning. To tell them all would bring disorder into their lives, for once exposed to truth, those not understanding develop hostility.

He was wise in his ways, as was Buddha, Zoroaster and many other Masters who have come to this earth for the purpose of giving their messages of truth to the unlearned and unlettered masses.

Yet, for your information, they are still with us

today to give the truth to all mankind. Yes, there are many here, though some do not show themselves to man. There are many who teach openly, and others who stay hidden in the deep recesses of the mountains, or those who walk among people in huge cities, not telling who they might be, but helping man in a way that is unknown to him!

Did you ever meet a beggar on the street who made you wonder at his strange eyes or his peculiar mannerisms? Care is needed in the examination of the ones who fit such a description for they could be ECK Masters in disguise, disguised in this particular way to bring a blessing to any they encounter. Watch for them in a store, on the streets, in the parks, or along the highways. Someone may approach you and ask for a small token of help. He could be the Living ECK Master. One of my experiences, while serving under Rebazar Tarzs, was that I found one of the ECK Masters in the guise of a beggar. I had been in difficulty for some time, and was very unhappy over the fact that nothing could be found to solve my problem.

On a particular afternoon while I was looking in a shop window a voice spoke from behind asking for money to purchase coffee. Turning I found a strange looking person of medium height. He wore old clothes, but they were neatly pressed, his face thin, well shaven, and ageless. What struck me most were his piercing eyes that bore deeply into me, giving rise to some strange feeling that I was standing in the presence of a great entity.

All the money I had at this time was a pair of quarters in my pocket. Taking out one I handed it to him, explaining that he could get coffee and a sandwich at a small tavern around the corner.

I added, "I've very little for times have been hard for me too!"

The beggar looked me in the eyes with his strange piercing gaze and replied, "You will have the blessings of the Sugmad at once. Do not worry!"

With that he turned and disappeared into the crowd. It was a few moments before I recovered from that statement and ran after him, but in that brief period he had completely vanished. It was only a few days later that my affairs took a turn for the better and my problem was solved.

The night after my problem had dissolved, the ECK Adept appeared to me in a dream. He said, "You are under my protection. I come to you to give you help. Whenever anything happens and you are discouraged and beaten by the world, I will come to you, in different guises, to help. Never worry again about life's problems on Earth."

This is one of the many incidents that I will give you which happened in my life, and which can happen in your life, if only you become aware of what is occurring around you.   Start

We meet the ECK Master constantly. He is everywhere, sometimes in disguise, at other times openly. It is not only that he is helping you materially, but unloosing the shackles of that which has put chains on your spirit and holds you to this world. By unfastening these chains he makes you a channel through which God may work.

We alone are responsible for our spiritual life, and our material beingness. A Master will tell you what and how to do the right things with the proper techniques, but he always leaves the doing to the individual. Since Soul is the final step in one's own becomingness, then it is up to Soul to create Its own course of action to the ultimate peak of all things, God.

Nobody can do it for you. If Soul is the effect of

something, then It must change this, take the initiative, and become cause. That and that alone! Soul can always be cause, can take care of Itself. Of course, It can be effect, but It must be knowing effect, never unknowing.

Always look at life in this way. Naturally we are constantly the effect of life, but to be effect, unknowingly, is a criminal offense against Soul.

Consider life in this manner. Since it gives back what we put into it, we must give only good to it. Good means God; it is only the long version of God. Abstract words like joy, happiness, and good have a scientific meaning. They represent in words the control of certain thought streams composed of the atoms which are best for the survival of Soul, whether It is living in the body or without one.

We can say that the Flute of God is actually that great Sound Current which Soul rides upon in Its return journey to Its true home. Soul must be in control of Its own destiny whether under the protection of the Master or God. This is always true, and of course, the Soul is God, Itself!

I am aware that there are many approaches to God. No one individual has a monopoly on these approaches. What Mary Baker Eddy used as an avenue to Truth would be completely awry with that used by the Master Saint Ramakrishna, founder of the Ramakrishna Mission, an order in the Vedanta religion of India; or what Moses or Sankara used in their respective philosophies; and even with that of the greatest Sufi Saint, Shamus-i-Tabriz, in ancient Persia.

So the whole truth is. And nothing more. It is that we must find our own way to God. There is no teacher, living or past, who can give us the actual understanding of truth. A teacher can only put our feet upon the

11

path and point the way. That is all. It is wholly dependent on the individual to make his way to truth.

When he learns, suddenly he finds out the secret of the ages, the simplest of all things. That each of us is truth. We are the living truth—the very embodiment of God. That is, we are each God, Itself. Rather, we are a part of the great whole of truth!

Perhaps you cannot grasp this point yet. Here is an example of how it was explained to me in its elementary form. The great ECK Master Fubbi Quantz gave me this clue by the use of only two words.

He told me in a very clear voice, "Just be!"

That is the key to all we have been talking about. Just be! For if we know that now we are at that point where we have always wanted to be, we will be there! Notice the reconstruction of the sentence. For if we know that now we are at this point, where we have always wanted to be, we will be here!

The two words, this and here, changed the whole meaning because we are never there, but always here, now. Here and now put us in the present moment. Nothing should be projected into space or into the future. Truly realize that this is not a course of action at all, but a positive action of being in the present. Being it now, we have succeeded in having truth. In being truth! Do you understand this?

Jesus proclaimed this in his great message to his disciples, especially directing his words to Peter, outside Bethany when he withered the fig tree. "What things soever ye desire, when ye pray, believe that ye receive *them,* and ye shall have *them.*"

When his words were later translated into print, the priests or monks used the word *believe,* but we now know that he meant certainty. Development of the science of thought has brought man to the realization that prayer is not as Jesus was said to have taught, but is a fact of knowing, without reservation, that we live in the eternal now. *End*

Yaubl Sacabi, residing in Agam Des, the spiritual city in the Himalayas, states that "all is here now!" We must be prepared to lay claim to it now.

Many teachers, saints, and Masters state it both strongly or mildly, but none are indifferent to this principle of life, which can be summed up as: "All that we want, or will ever desire, already exists. It depends upon our asking for it to bring it into the present moment!" *Start*

Truth is here, in this present moment, and we must seize it, hold it, and be it—truth itself!

How can we do otherwise?

In the course of my travels and studies of truth over the past thirty years, and the investigation of the works of hundreds of mystics, holy men, God seekers, religious leaders and philosophers, the search and study under living teachers, and those beyond this world in other planes, I have come to one conclusion— they are seeking the ultimate, that God which is beyond what we name the ECK, Spirit, Divine Consciousness, Prana, or whatever you want to call that high spiritual energy flowing through the worlds, both invisible and visible.

Of course we are dealing with an abstraction here for the layman, but for the seekers of truth, it is a genuine, living understanding reality; alive, and as fascinating as the tiny flower blooming by the roadside or the fresh face of a newborn child. They come to know where God is and what God is.

Under assumed names I have traveled many lands in this physical body and in my spiritual self. I have explored every realm of the cosmic worlds; visited other planets, universes, and worlds; talked with great spiritual teachers, Masters and saints; and mingled within the known spheres of all spiritual travelers. The very thought is staggering to the imagination for the average seeker can hardly think of life beyond the tiny universe in which he lives.

I have been compelled, yes, that word is used by the ECK Masters, to undergo great discipline to learn truth. In my past lives, I served under many teachers, including the great Pythagoras, Master in the Greek golden age; Milarepa, the Tibetan saint; the Mexican God, Quetzalcoatl; Shamus-i-Tabriz, the Sufi mystic; and hundreds of others. It was the Greek who gave me five years of silence, without the least spoken word.

Many words, things, and deeds will be declared on truth throughout this volume and other casebooks to follow. They will, perhaps, be jumbled at spots as my thoughts and ideas rush forth. My mind staggers when I think of the part I have played to bring out the lessons of the higher consciousness, what my past has been and what the present is. There is no future, of course, except what we intend to make of it.

The present is basically all. We operate only in the present moment. Not in the past, nor the future, but NOW! This is important to remember. Never forget this, for it is the basic cardinal point of the cosmic worlds.

I am going to give you a complete picture of my basic conception of the philosophy of life. It is as if I have opened a door and invited you into my house to see what is there for you to view.

At times you will be overwhelmed, perhaps confused, and will not want to face what is to come, but that is when you should put aside negative thoughts and bear the responsibility of listening, for as Jesus said, once you put your hands upon the plow handles, there is no turning back!

Truth is here now. It is up to you to take charge of yourself and to accept it now!

It is possible for everybody!

2

Symbols of the Princes

e have all lived for eternity whether in this universe or another, because eternity has no beginning or ending. It is all an endless circle as long as we live in this universe of time and space.

We have not realized that we are individuals, entirely separated from one another, who must take responsibility for our own actions.

As Soul, we have accepted a body and can live in it as long as we like. Usually we accept the mores laid down by society, that our life expectancy is from sixty to seventy years in this body.

Usually we think of ourselves as a part of the whole, and this is true in a sense. Yet it is not, when you look upon the world as a unity. As such we ourselves are the cause of this world and the conditions within it. Chaos comes because we have built it into our consciousness. The magnetic atmosphere gives back only that which is put into it by conscious thought.

Therefore, every man must look to himself for responsibility. One cannot go any further than this. Usually man's limited viewpoint is narrowed by the very fact that he does not wish to accept responsibility but attempts to have another take it for him.

There is a danger in attempting oneness with all, as one may so scatter one's attention that the condition called "scattered all over the universe" may occur and one becomes the many, instead of the singular one. By this I mean you may lose your own self-motivation by letting too much of yourself go astray. Let yourself be the individual until it is possible to rise high enough to live with self before attempting to be one with all.

In a way, man lives in two worlds. The outer life that man lives is limited, but the Prince of God lives in a boundless inner world. One can become a slave to the influences from without instead of being free, influenced from within as Soul.

Now you must remember that until coming into the awareness of "I AM THAT" or God Itself, you are still the Prince, the potential heir to the throne. Each of us must learn the responsibility of the throne which we, as individuals, will inherit someday, as well as the principle by which the King, Our Father, governs all His subjects.

Do you understand this simplicity? Savants, sages, rishis, saviors, munis, and avatars have expressed this idea to the peoples of this world. We are the offspring of the Eternal who must recognize Its Spirit in all men and greet them as part of the Eternal.

Each Soul desires to be the Prince, to live like the Prince. The heir to the throne knows his power, his position in life. He lives in confidence, leaning upon the support of his high estate, upon the knowledge that the King is his father.

Therefore, the principle involved here is, "We live and have our being in the Supreme Being." Lai Tsi, the Chinese ECK Master, said it this way, "We live and move and have our being in the Sugmad." Other savants state it in a slightly different vein. For instance, Jalal ad-Din ar-Rumi said, "Divine Grace is not limited by the conditions of ability, but ability, in fact, is conditioned by Divine Grace."

Being the Prince, the heir to the kingdom of heaven, we look to the symbol of God. Until we realize that truth is ourselves, that the individual is truth Itself, we are always seeking after something which cannot be grasped.

This realization of truth can be instantaneous. It need not depend upon years of struggle, working through the most diabolical chain ever put upon the neck of man, called karma. Ghaous Ali Shah Qulander, a Sufi mystic, once said, "Giving perfection to a disciple is a matter of a fraction of a second. A word in the ear is enough to lift a man at once from finiteness to infinity, and such a transformation is not dependent upon prayers or fasts."

Truth, in fact, can never be organized or encompassed by one or the many, for it does not lend itself to this modus operandi. Because of its peculiarity of action, those who attempt to organize it as churches, orders or institutions will eventually meet with failure.

However, the history of mankind, particularly in religions and philosophies, proves this statement. Take a backward glance through history and you will find that the organized religious groups and institutions on this Earth planet ran only a few hundred years, a small cycle of time in comparison with the trillion of years of its existence, then passed into oblivion. Why?

For the simple reason that unless the Living ECK Master endows an organization with his vitality, then the institution or group will not continue for any length

19

of time. Look at the orthodox order of religions who use their holy book as the living master. These are dead religions. So is metaphysics and many others that you may care to look up.

Examine the time of Guru Nanak, founder of the Sikh religion. He had marvelous powers, one of which was to transfer his power to others. He could move his physical body through space and raise the consciousness of his followers so that they were able to see their past and future and have the same understanding of God as he. Many saints possessed similar powers. However, we do not hear much about them for the reason that the authorities of the churches and organized religions have not written and will not write about them.

I'd like to continue this subject and state that the ECK power is the Knower. It is the positive, the objective side of life that we see reflected in those with balanced emotional responses. This power is reflected through cheerfulness, enthusiasm, action, and love. The mind, of itself, is only a repository of collected impressions. The power that actuates the body and mind is the ECK power.

However, the ECK power can only give us what we take and since the taking is of our own free will, an act of consciousness, we must be actively aware of the presence of our desire. We must know that the gift is made even before we see it. Consciousness must receive the gift before it comes into manifestation on this physical plane.

As the Princes of God, heirs to the throne of the Supreme Being, we must be consciously aware that we can take what is desired from Spirit, the God power.

Incidentally, there are four parts of man, the individual: Spirit, Soul, mind, and body. The mortal self is never able to do anything. It is the ECK Spirit that does everything, controlled by Soul. Unless Soul is conscious of what It does and works toward a goal, using Spirit as Its means of endeavor, then It will never reach the throne of the Father.

What is the symbol of the Princes? That symbol is truth. The living truth of which every man and being on this earth is composed. Truth is within every man, as is God the Omnipresent, working through each and all.

Truth is the symbol of the Princes. It is composed of three parts. These are: truth, nobility, and aesthetics. The higher one climbs the ladder toward emotional balance, the closer he comes to truth; and the more he sees of beauty in all, the more noble he becomes.

In chapter 7 of the book of Numbers in the Old Testament, it is related that the princes of the twelve tribes of Israel presented their gifts to be offered to God. Moses accepted them for he was the Messenger of the Divine Being who dedicated them at the Altar. We have evolved since that day, until now there is no intermediator between ourselves and God. We, the Princes, can recognize ourselves and go directly to God with our requests. The Sugmad will never deny Its sons their rightful place and heritage.

None of us differ as beings in this universe in the amount of power we possess—our only difference is the amount of power we realize we have, and use. Until man realizes this and masters himself he cannot hope to exert influence beyond himself. Unfoldment can be swift or slow; it depends upon the realization of the power within, and this takes us back to the point made on a previous page. That is, Spirit can give us only what we take. This is the way of the ECK power in this universe, and there is no other way. It depends upon our consciousness to act in this manner, not by an act of violence or a strong determination of the will.

Realization in the consciousness is very necessary; we must know that it is there before it appears to us.

Does this seem too simple? In truth, it is simple.

There is no complexity in it at all. It is being certain of receiving. The act of knowing that it is there is the greatest and most important thing in the world. For this is how awareness is brought about.

Why then should we study awareness?

Awareness is the movement of the inner being to know. This has to do with making use of the faculties for seeing and knowing.

Some people may be compared to Don Quixote who was of noble intention, yet muddled in mind, who tilted at windmills, saw enemies where none existed, and recognized ignorant peasant girls as princesses.

It is a matter of consciousness, the factor of awareness, which makes one know of life. Those who dwell and make their livelihood in the field of thought have an average I.Q. of 145. This is a level on which the Princes dwell and have their being. They are the heirs to the throne who must be alert to their own welfare and attitude toward life.

Passing from the lower concepts of life we come into our first understanding of the universe and may find its laws now seem quite topsy-turvy; we feel an urge to adopt or find a new philosophy for stability's sake. In doing so, there lies a danger.

Puffed up with a little knowledge and power gained, one becomes vain; and once vanity seizes him, complete confusion follows. Knowledge is applied wrongly, and the result can be ruin.

All his achievements, his possessions, his status in the eyes of the world can be destroyed at one sweep, save Soul. Soul, then, can rise like the phoenix from the ashes of life's annihilation, be stronger and better for the trials which It has passed, can rebuild life, career, and everything else anew and be greater than before.

It is dangerous for those individuals who use the spiritual power improperly. Like the Prodigal Son, they can squander their inheritance. However, properly applied with moral courage and daring, one can use the occult secrets on the mundane plane.

We can go only so far with impunity. Powers come fairly easy; knowledge seems to flow in on us, but the moment we start using these powers in the wrong way, they turn on us and raze our achievements to the ground.

Thus we become our own executioners and bring about our ruin through ambition allied with vanity. It is man's vanity in the powers he has learned that is the two-edged sword. There he is perched on a lofty tower, above his fellowmen, because he has learned certain spiritual secrets. The world, he thinks, is his private oyster. He will wrench from it the pearl he desires and impose his own will upon it.

Thus he comes into conflict with the secret laws. They help man to soar, but his intention must be to make this world a better place. These laws can and will raise him to the zenith of power if he holds this ideal before his vision. But once let him falter in his dedication to the Sugmad, the King upon the Throne; once let him put himself and self-glorification before the ideal of helping the world, or as Jesus put it, being about his Father's work, and these same powers in this universe will topple him to utter ruin.

The Prince must be above these secret laws of this

23

world, for they have been established by those governing the universe in which he lives. This is the secret. Are you governed by the laws laid down by Souls who have designated themselves as the governing power? Are you willing to be controlled by them?

These laws are very subtle for they seek out the weakness in every man so as to destroy him. The leaders in the East know the powers of the secret laws and can turn them on the West when in danger. Strangely, those in the West have not yet recognized the subtle dangers of the East and Easterners who have used these laws of the universe for centuries.

That individual who is greedy for riches is allowed to amass them; then possession of those riches becomes the sword that strikes him down. With millions at his command, he is often placed in a position where no sum of money can help him. A man, thus, must face his own weakness and conquer it or be conquered by it. If the latter, then he has been found wanting. Those who are not defeated rise from the depths to soar again, to rebuild life anew, and here they have the help of the Sugmad.

The power of God can be compared to a speeding train. Brake it suddenly to a dead stop, and the coaches telescope. Stop short of your true goal as a Prince of God, forget the symbol of the Princes, the uplifting of humanity, and the bettering of the world; and you have attempted to renege on your responsibilities. The answer is swift and deadly for the higher you climb, the harder you will fall.

The symbol of the Princes is not a secret hidden behind locked doors, for the power of God, which is in reality the symbol which all men use to gain mastership over all things, is the great builder of life. That and nothing more.

(handwritten: What does this mean)

The Svetasvatara Upanishad says: "Just as the mirror cleansed of its impurities becomes lustrous and reflects a bright image, even thus does the God seeker behold himself at the height of his spiritual transport and attain the goal of his endeavor."

This is what Sudar Singh spoke of in his dialogues. "We must become the conscious Co-workers with God."

Once man is freed of his imbalances, he inherits the throne and does his work for the whole.

Now we turn to the power flows which are man's concerns while living in this world. When I speak of man, I am referring to the Soul of man, the "I AM," the Atman, whatever name you want to call It.

One of Newton's laws of motion in physics states that for every action there is an equal and opposite reaction. For every flow of energy there is, and must be, a counterflow. This is what we call cause and effect.

(handwritten margin: Positive / Negative)

A person is usually one or the other. He is being, and being is always an aspect of negative and positive. When a person is cause he is being positive. When he is effect, he is being negative.

(handwritten margin: Explain this)

To be more explicit, being positive is a power flow outward, toward the good of the whole. Being negative is a power flow inward, toward the good of parts, one or a few. This is the meaning of unselfish and selfish, of positive and negative.

In the first part of this chapter I spoke of this: "The power of God gives only what we take." Being positive means to be cause, to take as much of the power for use as we desire knowingly. Being negative means that we are not partaking of the power knowingly, and generally we are the receptor.

Cause and effect work together. Only when desiring something, does one set up a cause and receive it.

It is necessary to use the subtle law of the universe in the following manner. We must willingly be effect in order to get the fulfillment of our desire, for the "consciousness must receive the gift."

It is simple: to be cause, to assume the positive outlook over anything, or be able to receive, one must contribute to whatever is contributing to him; in other words, one must cooperate and be flexible in changing and balancing the power flow around him.

Instead of having the "power flow" pour toward you, it can be reversed whenever you desire, and you can have it flow outward toward the original cause-point.

This may be done by prototypes. These prototypes, visualizations or mental pictures, must be of the time of the event. If you read a book, your visualization must be of the events created by the author. You must see him writing that particular scene; see the words being put upon the paper in his typewriter.

If you actually understand this action, you realize that you can use the same technique in any of the arts—music, sculpture, modeling, stage plays, painting, business negotiations, or anything that life presents to you as a situation, circumstance, or problem in which you regard yourself as the effect.

Can you visualize Mozart composing one of his great masterpieces, while you are listening to a recording of his works; or Dickens, working on his immortal book *David Copperfield*? Do this with anything you desire, and after a while it will become a part of you.

This is when you begin to cleanse the tablets of the mind of any errata so that you can receive truths of absolute transcendence. The accumulation of falseness must be taken from the Atman, the Soul, to enable It to shine forth in Its own resplendence.

Of course, we are dealing with energy in space. That is all there is to this phenomenon. Nothing more. We must work toward the end of keeping effect, the negativeness, from depositing accumulations of falseness as unnatural additions to the body. If we do not do this, we will become bound and inhibited by this material which produces reactive patterns that are bothersome to us.

With this understanding that you have gained, we go back to the symbol of the Prince. The Prince is always in a knowing state of mind seeking his goal of truth, nobility and aesthetics. At this present stage he does not know that in order to succeed at his goal, he must be these; he must become these qualities of God.

These qualities are from the throne of the Supreme Being; they are the arms and the seat upon which the power is placed and from which It flows. Therefore, the symbol of the Prince is the throne; and it is made of these qualities, until he is seated on it to reign. He becomes these qualities before he is placed upon his Father's throne to receive the kingship. We can each become the King, not in succession, but at the same time. For within each of us is a kingdom to rule.

Soul acquires special knowledge as It journeys through life, casting off falseness, and getting closer to the state of being free. At every stage It feels that It takes control and can dominate all the experiences that It receives. This is described by some mystics who have gone to other planes, who have gained control over the planes through which they have passed.

Those who make a mystery of life, who attempt to keep it hidden from their fellowmen, create religions and philosophies. This is not too difficult. The thing least known and most mysterious to man is his own

27

being. Orthodox psychology is occupied with the obvious thoughts and emotions of man, yet his very essence, the "I" to whom these experiences happen, remains beyond its reach.

Many religions have hidden their teachings under the veil of symbols. This was done by the clergy of those philosophies so that the layman would always be under the control of religious orders, and to keep from exposing themselves to the dangers of torture and death.

However, today the secret doctrine is spoken openly. Great sages make it the keynote of their teachings. In the welter of words which one can find in the libraries, or for sale in the bookstores, there are only a few occult theories that are of any help in the quest for self-knowledge. Yes, there are only a handful that have certain practical use in understanding the world of relativity, the world in which one is compelled to live.

One of these is the Cabala, the Jewish mystical teaching of that ancient religion of Judea. Its theory consists of only inner planes, upon which there exists a group of beings who play an important role in the material life of humanity and the individual fate of men. Their existence is as real as the material world about you. The principle that exists here is simply: "As above, so below!"

This is one of the greatest principles ever given in the field of thought. It means that whatever you think is bound to be yours, be it good, bad, or indifferent. The outer world is manifested from the emanations made by Soul; the general results are caused by their inner thinking. The God power is based upon wavelengths, and indeed there is no above nor below when acting outside of space. We think in terms of operating on various wavelengths through the power of thought.

Let us advance this thought further. Whatever we think, we are. Rebazar Tarzs, Kabir, Guru Nanak, St. Paul, Fubbi Quantz, Zoroaster, Buddha, Tulsi Das, and many other Masters and savants have told us this time and again.

Here is a simple illustration: You are acquainted with the way modeling clay can be formed into any shape you desire? You know how to make an impression on it by laying a coin or a key on the clay and pressing it? You produce a perfect reproduction in reverse on the clay. If the reproduction were filled with liquid plaster and allowed to harden, you would then be able to lift out an exact copy of the coin or key.

This is how it is as one uses the visual powers of the mind in harmony with the God powers. By jelling a clear image or impression of what you desire and holding it clearly every day, you make an impression on the God power.

Into this hollow thus formed, the everpresent, interpenetrating divine power flows, like the liquid plaster, and presently you have the perfect reproduction of what you held in mind. Remember that this is what happens when you think—so think of what you wish to be produced in your life. Here is an eternal, unchanging process that always works.

Lao-tzu, the Chinese teacher, says: "Once grasp the great form without form, and you roam where you will with no evil to fear; calm, peaceful, and at ease."

The form without form, the divine ECK, suggests the Platonic form or idea, the archetype; the all-embracing form or idea in which things exist potentially until realized in the material, the actual outer world.

The symbol of the Princes then is the positive way of life emerging from the development of true

29

maturity of mind and experience derived from daily education. It is based upon certain principles of life, taken out of positive and negative concepts. They are:

POSITIVE	NEGATIVE
Progressive	Retrogressive
Light	Dark
Heat	Cold
Abstract	Concrete
Spirit	Matter
Growth	Decay
Theory	Fact
Innovation	Reaction
Intellect	Emotion
Free Will	Fatalism
Independence	Dependence
Master	Slave
Faith-Courage	Doubt-Fear
Success	Failure
Concept	Form

So you see the Princes dwell in the positive attitude at all times. They have become stable in this type of thinking and have set an archetype of enthusiasm, into which the divine power flows and brings forth the perfect reproduction which is generally of the higher nature of man.

Let yourself accept the true heritage of what God has offered you—Sonship in His Kingdom. You are the Prince of the Throne, the Son of God.

3

Purification of the Princes

here is an intelligence running through the entire cosmic universe expressing itself in all the varied forms of life. It is observed in every animated action and appears in forms of animated life up through the highest spiritual level.

We can only prove that such a power exists by finding it in all life. To be able to make such an observation, we, the Princes, who are the Sons of God, must possess the realization of that intelligence or power.

Descartes said, "I think, therefore I am," and with this statement, he announced the philosophy of the analytical mind of man. If you make this observation you demonstrate the two parts of the whole; first, the material or exterior side of man, and second existence, or what we call survival.

That man goes through a purification before coming into his own Godhead is well known to all. In the beginning he was pure. As Soul, he came into this world without any excess baggage, but then he created a lower mind. When he ceased to monitor it, it began to outcreate him, and this became his downfall.

Psychology calls it the subconscious mind, and Christianity says it is the devil. All religions and philosophies have a name for this part of man that began to outcreate Soul upon its arrival in this universe.

This part of man which began to outcreate Soul in the beginning still does so today. Until he is aware of this and looks to Soul as the prime creator, man will always lean upon something else to do for him and will be its effect.

One must set out to break the fixed desires of his own nature. These desires have been established in the subconscious mind over a period of many incarnations. They retard one's growth and progress toward becoming a Master. You must first find the nature of their origin and proceed from there.

Of course, it is unwise for one to tamper with his own subconscious mind without first having knowledge of its nature. Mind makes for the complexity of man. The individual personality is a composite of expressed desires. We will discover there really is no way of getting rid of any of our desires made in the past, whether they are considered good or bad, but once the individual recognizes their meaning, he can begin to modify and take control of them, instead of having them control him.

Life is not built on mistakes; success in life comes from being able to recognize that one has committed an error and subsequently accepting the responsibility for rectifying it. The sure way to fail is contained in the fear of failure.

When one dwells in the positive mind, he is the master; in the negative mind, he is the slave. The negative state of the subconscious mind is that of the slave. Here one is subject to the laws of the material universe, the world of matter, energy, space, and time.

The goal of all God seekers is to become stable in the positive state.

The principles of these two sides of the universe are: the positive—the masculine, or the light, and the negative—the feminine, or the dark. This Law of Polarity, the Law of Opposites, is found wherever one goes in this universe. One can be conscious of its existence as long as one remains aware of these principles.

There are two kinds of teachers: those who know little about the subconscious and present it in the light that might be said to represent the channel through which we must work in order to reach our goal in becoming a Co-worker with God, and those who say that the path lies in direct contact with the power itself. The latter follow no system, but make an effort toward Self-Realization without using any aids.

A good test of this is shown in the stock answers received from those teachers who are ignorant. They will generally answer a disciple who is in trouble with comments such as: "God will take care of everything. Put your faith in God." This type of teacher will carefully explain that it is your karma being worked out. Too many want to accept this theory because it relieves them of responsibility. It is accepted because it gives them the feeling of being a martyr. In their opinion God has tested them.

A real teacher does very little for the individual, except point the way. The greatest flaw that we have, as students of the Divine Science, is to expect results to come from outside ourselves. Instead, they always come from within the individual who makes an effort toward using the God power.

For those who seek a goal, the common complaint is delay. "If I am God," one says, "then why can't it be realized?"

Usually because one is not willing to accept what he is. By not doing so, the individual closes himself to the higher planes from which the divine blessings flow. When he learns this, does an about-face, and starts anew, he gains his goal.

It is seldom that an obstacle has anything to do with a goal or desire, but tension does. Tension is almost always the cause of delay. Whenever one feels tense, desperately anxious about something, his contact with the God power is lessened, for tension fastens the consciousness on the plane of illusion, instead of on the plane of what is possible. One is apt to be visualizing the lack of what is desired, rather than what is desired.

The solution is to make contact with the God power, to relax in God and let God's blessings flow. We have free will to make our own choices. We are at liberty to grow into the knowledge of our powers as the Prince and heir of God, or not. And it will happen, despite centuries of subtle, often hidden unbelief of fixed desires.

The solution to every desire and problem that man has comes through his consciousness. Others can strengthen and encourage us, but it is our own consciousness that receives the gift. If we cannot solve the difficulty at hand, it is because of something within us. We are working with hope and not faith.

Faith is developed by seeking a greater understanding of God, and using it unwaveringly. Actual faith enables one to cooperate with God in a calm manner. Purifying the self and clearing away the obstacles present in the consciousness is the next step. One has to understand the unchangeable working of truth and, finally, to cooperate fearlessly and faithfully with truth.

34

Those who are ready to accept their discipleship, to step into their true heritage, are invited by the Master to do so. This is often done in a strange way. When the Master says, "Follow me," he does so to one who is able and ready to go wherever He is going—which can be into an inner plane.

Do you remember the story in the Bible of the man who came to Jesus and said that wherever Jesus went he would go too? And Jesus answered, saying that the foxes have holes and the birds of the air have nests; but the Son of man had nowhere to lay his head.

Jesus was gently telling this man that he was not ready to follow, but immediately he turned to one of the disciples and said, "Follow me."

The disciple was to follow the Master into the world where there were no established, visible homes, but where Soul could wander at will. The first man was not able to follow into this inner plane, but the other disciple had the understanding and ability. However, even though he might have been able to follow, he hesitated. The outer consciousness, the world and its ties, attracted him. Actually the same situation existed with the disciple that Jesus invited to go with him as with the other man.

Then Jesus said: "No man, having put his hand to the plough, and looking back, is fit for the kingdom of God." This is reported in Luke 9:62. What he meant was that such a person is not fit to enter into the consciousness of God within one.

This meant that the first man who wanted to follow Jesus was locked in the outer consciousness of the world. He believed only in those things that he could see and had little faith in his ability to create and to do mighty works by himself in the realm of the invisible. He wanted to follow the Master everywhere, but

Jesus frequently went into a state of such high consciousness that he could even elude the grasp of men who sought to capture him in crowds.

He had no home then, even one as humble as the foxes and birds, but roamed the cosmic worlds at will. The first man could not follow Jesus there. The disciple could, for he was a disciple of the Master and had been trained, yet he drew back from following and doing mighty works of faith.

You should be able to follow and receive the power for mighty works. Jesus said to those who followed him so long ago that he had given them the power.

The official moralists, like those who followed the pseudomasters, have laid down rules for the salvation of Soul which are wrong. They advise us to never relax our strenuousness. "Be vigilant, day and night. Hold your passive tendencies in check; shrink from no effort; keep your will always bent."

This conscious effort leads to nothing but failure and vexation by those who attempt it. It makes them confused. Their tense and determined attitude becomes an intolerable thing to them, a fever and torment.

The way to success in God Consciousness lies in giving up the feeling of need, letting go your hold, resigning the care of your destiny to God; being genuinely indifferent to what becomes of all. You will not only gain a perfect inner relief, but often the particular things you sincerely thought you were renouncing. This is salvation through self-renunciation, the dying to be truly reborn. To get to it, a critical point must be passed, a corner turned within. Something must give way, a native hardness must break down and liquefy. This event is frequently sudden and natural, and leaves one with the impression that he has received the blessings of God.

36

This significant event proves to be the fundamental experience in the individual which turns him away from the outer consciousness to the viewpoint of the Real Self. This divides the religious from the moralists, and the true Godman from the religious. With those who undergo this experience in its fullness, there is no doubt of its reality. They know, for in giving up the tension of their personal will, they have actually felt the Higher Power.

There is a story of the man who found himself at night slipping down the side of a precipice. He caught a branch which stopped his fall, and remained clinging to it in misery for hours. Finally his fingers lost their hold, and with death in mind, he let himself drop. He fell just six inches. If he had given up the struggle earlier, his agony would have been spared. As the Earth received him, so will the ECK power receive us if we release absolute faith to It and give up the subconscious habit of relying on personal strength, with its precautions that cannot shelter and safeguard that which it never saves.

Man does not live by bread alone. He lives also upon the Spirit life. He is a conscious being and has to know himself to live in God Consciousness. Man as a conscious entity expresses himself through mind and the physical body. Unless his consciousness is liberated from the bondage of mind and matter, he cannot have knowledge of self and of God. If his mind is turned to the physical body and its needs, he becomes earthly. The inevitable results are jealousies and strifes. But if his mind is directed toward Soul, it becomes spiritual and the result is love and peace.

All ECK Masters turn man's attention to the purification of the heart. If we want to change the outside, we should change our hearts first, because out of the

37

abundance of heart a man speaks. Purity in thought, word and deed is what is required. Consider then how to conquer the mind and purify the heart. Man is composed of body, mind, and Soul. We have to develop all around. But unknowingly, the mind and body depend on Soul, of which the world knows very little or nothing. "For what shall it profit a man, if he gains the possession of the whole world and loses his Soul?"

All Masters of earlier days exhorted us to know ourselves. To know ourselves we have to rise above the body consciousness by practical self-analysis. Intellectual people fail badly where the practical side is concerned. To be born anew is to rise above the body consciousness by practical self-analysis in order to enable one to know himself and the Sugmad, which is another name for God. Gopal Das says the same thing: "Learn to die a hundred times daily, not once." We must know how to rise above the body consciousness so as to know who we are, and what we are. Intellectually we know much about it, but practically, we know little or nothing. It is a matter of rising above the body consciousness and opening the eye of Soul. Then we see the Light of God that which we have forgotten from past incarnations.

We have forgotten our mastership of life. Can we rise above the body consciousness? Can we leave the body and then return to it? These are teachings given by almost all the Masters of the ages, whether they come in one country or another. To achieve this, man must lead an ethical life. This is a stepping-stone to spirituality. Jesus said, "Blessed are the pure in heart for they shall see God." Rebazar Tarzs said, "Be pure so that truth may be known."

The basic principle in this study of purification is learning relaxation from all tension. This I have discussed before, and I will continue to come back to the subject.

The great law of the universe is "Love one another." Every teacher has told us this. Why? Simply because when we love others, our heart and consciousness are relaxed, and our attention is taken off the self. What happens then? We relax when we forget ourselves. That is the natural and universally recognized result. A tense person is wrapped up in himself or his immediate family—what he is feeling and thinking, what has happened to him in the past or will happen to him in the future or what other people are thinking of him. But if that person can be persuaded to forget himself, he relaxes immediately. Now what does tenseness do to one? It grips; it causes a stranglehold to be put on the channels within; it cuts off supply. God and the love of others is cut off. Watch a tense person and see the rigid muscles, the tight grip, the jerky movements, the deep lines of the facial muscles. It is useless for such a person to relax physically while still centering the mind on the self, for he will still be tense mentally. The stranglehold will be there every minute, day and night.

Signs of such tenseness are evident in most of us. Those who seek God and fail often feel that it is not their own fault, that the approach is wrong. There is a feeling of injustice, of having to struggle for something that should be given freely because of one's good work and great need. However, one who is in this position is not looking very closely at himself. There is a focal point for this delay; a cause for the delay in reaching God. When one loves another as himself, his attention is focused outward. He is therefore relaxed. There is no stranglehold within. Then he becomes a channel for the power, and often demonstrates his conscious union with God. Yet when he asks for

39

something for himself, his attention is focused inwardly. He instantly becomes tense and feels that it is a great struggle to get that which he desires.

One must relax utterly, then the divine ECK power flows through. There are two principles involved here. To project our energy outward, and to love our neighbor as ourselves.

The scientific factors involved are: As Soul, we have the power to create—using time, space, matter, and energy. Here again is a polarity, a pulsation, a flow that works in two ways: an outward flow from the "I" which is called Soul; and an inflow, from others upon the "I"—the positive and the negative.

The outflow is the creative energy. It enables Soul to be cause, to make Its own creations. This is why the mystics proclaim the love of God as the greatest of all principles: To love God so wholeheartedly that the consciousness is taken off the self and centered on God. The outflow of creative energy is so great that there is no room for struggle here, no space for the feeling of injustice. There is only the giving of good feeling, smoothly and uninterruptedly. This is the technique of purification of the Princes.

A Prince knowing that he is to inherit his father's Kingdom does not fasten his attention upon himself, causing tension, but yields his whole consciousness to his father's affairs.

The Prince knows that the fact of the sun's ray upon the earth is proof of the existence of the sun. So is the fact of his life here a proof of the existence of the All-Life. The ray of sunshine is not the sun but a projection of its substance. It is sustained by the sun itself. This, the Prince knows, is true of himself, for he is a projection of the substance of God, and is sustained by God.

Then he is purified. He is ready to yield his whole consciousness to God, and to ask God to fulfill his needs. Yet these needs do not now fasten his attention on himself and cause tenseness. They seem outside himself, as though they were the needs of another person, while he, himself, is one with the very universe itself, since he is a part of God.

Now the inflow works in reverse. When one is introverted he is looking at himself. The symptoms of those who are introverted are sleepiness and unconsciousness in regard to the environment. God, or Light, is the giver of life. Soul lives by Light, yet Light is often confused with knowledge. When there is no Light, Soul puts the body to sleep and there is a denial of reality. This means that one falls into the habit of regarding everything as a mystery. Match this with a dwindling power to be effective, and you will have total introversion. Have you ever seen anyone who was totally ineffectual and seemed to be the complete effect of anything around him? Persons who are caught up in this terrible state of being will dramatize their own darkness and will resent anything. They will try to dramatize everything that is near them and may become very destructive.

Soul manufactures Its own cage. The more introverted a person is, the more dangerous he is to himself, as well as to others. If he stays within his consciousness, he thinks he is inside something but is not sure what it is. He is so introverted that nothing else exists and the universe is lost to him.

It is easy to introvert another being. Getting him to look at himself introverts him. He becomes an introverted machine. Looking out from the personal viewpoint and back again at himself is the way of introversion. That is why when we keep looking at mind pictures we are looking at the backwash of energy upon ourselves. Soul often keeps Itself trapped in introversion by Its own desires, mental pictures, and self-imposed restrictions. Still one doesn't get out of things until he gets into them and takes part in them. Reexperience and practice getting into things, and you may break your own trap.

Soul falls in upon Itself because It is creating negative inflow. It is extroverted because It wants to be and is willing to be outside Its consciousness. When you inhibit your connection with your environment, you become introverted and will no longer face reality. To handle life, to be responsible for things is to be close to reality and creativity.

In our complex society today, we have money as a means to have things. No longer are we creative in the same sense as those who lived in a frontier society, where when things were needed, imagination was used to build or create them. Our present society has caused us to go from self-reliance to thoughtless buying. We are provided with ways to waste money, and the cost of this has given us a double standard. Quantity enters into this idea—to have just enough, too little, or too much are states of mind we often express. To have a lot is to exceed enough, and to have too little is scarcity. All is built around one's idea of quantity. Having more than enough or not enough can define how much introversion there is. However, introversion depends upon how little there is. Often Soul forces Itself into being extroverted by not having enough. It must go out to get it, extending Itself where It doesn't wish to extend. This is concerned with the consciousness— that which is all the thoughts and feelings of the individual, his state of awareness.

Soul is that which is the consciousness, the entity,

the beingness which is aware of Itself. It is very easy for Soul to confuse this awareness of being aware with the illusive and dreamlike mental processes and physical movements of daily living. When this loss of being aware is complete, the person's fondest belief is that he is a body.

Even when we have arrived at a state where we know that each of us has a spark of consciousness, we are still below the mark that Buddha called Bodhisattva, or Christ mind. We are all trying to reach the Mahanta consciousness, which is the highest of all states. We have self-knowledge when in this state of higher being, we can create energy at will, and handle, control, erase, or recreate as we desire. At this stage, Soul, instead of doing away with all the things It had been in conflict with, discovers It is capable of manipulating them. It discovers that It only thought It had to be in conflict with them. It learns judgment.

Soul's basic ability is survival, yet Its creations are destroyable, and confusing Itself with Its creations, It thinks and believes that it has to have or do certain things in order to survive. Anxiety becomes so great in regard to surviving that It believes It must have special things to do in order to survive. Soul is very unhappy unless It has some special personal problem, different from all other problems to wrestle with, giving It a false sense that if It has this very special problem It must be surviving.

Ability never changes, but willingness to exert does. When you are doing things with little or no interest and affection for the thing you are doing, your effort will fail. Maybe not immediately but sooner or later you will, so to speak, fall flat on your face. In this condition you are unwilling to be responsible for the things you are doing. Do too much of this, and you will

43

drive yourself into boredom and apathy and your communication with those about you and with your environment will be at a very low level.

People interested in control (dictators) know this and use work as a means to manipulate the masses.

Control is believed to be a slave master. We get involved in thinking this because at least once, and usually more times, we have failed to control something and decided that all we needed was more control. Again failing, we said that control was a negative principle, straight out of the subconscious mind. The real success in dealing with others is not control but the granting of freedom of mind, thinking, and action, and accepting others as independent beings.

This leads us into a brief study of the mind so that you may know more about it in the course of knowing yourself. The mind is merely a mechanism of the human being which stores up mental image pictures.

The mind is really a structure of mental images and machinery upon which the individual, who has not developed himself into acting of himself, is dependent for his opinions and ideas.

The mind is composed of complete mental pictures of various sizes, shapes, and conditions. The whole mental machine is only pictures. The mind stores patterns of thought, which when stimulated echo the information and appear to be alive.

The activity of the mind is terribly complicated; when thinking about this activity one sees but a confusion of pictures, records, and seemingly meaningless juxtapositions of recorded events. However, by analogy, it is simple to understand.

The mind may be considered like a phonograph recording. It won't play unless the urge, which is the stimulation, gets one to place the needle on the record.

The analytical part of the mind controls the tracking of the needle on the platter and when the record is playing in the groove, the recording is clear. But when the record is worn or the grooves filled in, the result is vague and indistinct and even skipping about on the record can occur.

If you have too little happening to you, you will cling too tightly to what you have. In fact, you will covet these few experiences so much that the recordings of them will begin to collapse one upon the other to the point where they will be so crowded together and will seem so dense they will appear as one picture and almost totally black. You will lose control and not be able to separate the pictures into separate recordings of events.

When the mind is in control of Soul, it is not a sane condition, and no one will ever succeed while being controlled by this inferior influence. Soul is the causative source and unless It is to some degree a conscious cause, It becomes lazy. Soul says to Itself, "Why think, everything is doing my thinking for me," and the next thing you know It ceases to influence the mind at all.

The mind is a simple machine capable of producing a fantastic abundance of mental phenomena. It does so by correlations, interpretations, comparisons, and the subsequent rerelations of significance produced. All of which seems to be thinking based on new thoughts and new experiences but actually is merely the computation of mental pictures and concepts on an I-am-supposed-to-do basis. When the mind goes into action it seems to be taking certain pertinent facts from the realism of existence. One of the basic purposes in having a mind is to provide a storehouse of information. It makes pictures and files them away. Becoming lazy, Soul even accepts secondhand incidents, actions, and drama, for they are better than none at all. This seems to be one of the facts detrimental to Soul.

We ought to try to lead exciting, stimulating lives rich in experience and to at least attempt to monitor our mental machinery.

The exact working of this machinery depends on association and differentiation. When the reasoning mind identifies everything with everything to get its patterns and responses, it becomes reactive. Soul no longer has association. This is what we call dissociation. Association and differentiation are two basic functions in the mind. The mind differentiates; it compares. Oppositely, it conceives similarities. A mind in good shape doesn't identify. When association becomes identification there results a lack of objects, a lack of incidents, a lack of experiences, a lack of things with which to function in life. Do not think that overwork all by itself can produce a mental condition, for if one is not busy, one will soon long for a time to be busy. If worried about a mental-image picture, one is busy, but these things are usually automatic and never have any life in them. However, if you create incidents, you are the cause-source point.

A restimulated incident is held in place by its authenticity, but this isn't all. Rare incidents are apt to stick with us. Scarcity and spontaneity will also hold incidents in place. The mind, as I said before, is a mechanism which is used to dealing with problems of the present by making available in the present its storehouse of experience and pictures. The amount of change and motion an individual needs is determined by his scarcity and abundance.

Another part of the mind is the body. This is the final remaining part. One's body is the solid appendage which makes a person recognizable. The connection between the body and Soul is the mind which is monitored by Soul. The body is subject to this connection, but it is not actually possible to change a body without changing other things. If you wish to make a permanent change of any kind in the body, then you have to change the mental structure. It is held together by what I call space points. This structure of the body is more easily influenced than Soul. Thus we find the surrounding universe influencing the body and mind, but not necessarily Soul.

It is possible to know yourself and rise above this body and mind consciousness. You are not the body, nor the mind, nor the faculties of sensation, but Soul Itself. Unless you know that you are the Prince and know what your relationship with God and all creation is, you cannot be at peace and inherit the Throne of the Father. So as it is said by one of the great saints, "Instead of preaching to others, we should start preaching to ourselves." End

We should love God, and as God resides in all hearts, we should learn to love all humanity and all creation that exists. If we do, all will go well. The true spiritual man looks to the God present in all hearts. He works from that level. The more persons there are like this in the world, the greater will be the spiritual environment and love for one another.

Once truth becomes a part of you, a part of your consciousness, a part of your outlook on life, then wonderful changes take place. However busy one might be, the true self goes on working, drawing to Itself the right experiences and the right things, attracting all that is desirable in life. It is not true that individuals succeed because they have leisure time, for those who are the most busy take divine truth into their deepest consciousness.

The whole point is not how busy one might be, but how deeply he has taken divine truth into his consciousness. It works for him, day and night, in whatever work he is engaged.

It is important that you see that no effect can be produced without adequate cause. If truth is set before us, explaining the causes and exhibiting the full measure of the effects, we have deep knowledge.

Gradually we come to the knowledge that thought possesses creative power, and that creative power is Spirit. This is the whole foundation for that into which the Princes, upon becoming purified, grow.

Thought, pure mental action, is the only possible source from which existing creation could ever have come into manifestation at all. This is the truth which we all seek, and grow into through the knowledge of possessing the power.

The Princes are the creators of the universe, the worlds and the existing forms in them.

The purification of the Princes is necessary, exacting, and true. It gives the power of freedom, creativeness, and ability.

It is the necessary growth for the next step to become God; that step is accepting the Godhood for that is what every Prince aspires to and is trained to be.

4

The Promises of the Prophet

*R*unning through the holy scriptures of the world there is found the golden thread of promises made by the prophets and saviors who were the light of these ages.

The divine promises have puzzled thinking people in every period of history, for while they speak of love, they speak also of wrath. How can the two be reconciled?

The divine promises are given in the Voice of the Everlasting Law. God put this law into action at the beginning of this universe. Within this universe, and many other universes, also, it is the Law of Cause and Effect. "Whatsoever a man soweth, that shall he also reap." This law is a just and logical one, and part of the great inheritance of man, who is God's heir. Whatsoever God has sown on earth by the power of Its divine thought, has grown into visible reality. Whatsoever man "sows" as the offspring and heir of God, comes into visible reality, also. God's thoughts are infinite; man's are finite, but both are operating under the same divinely appointed law.

Within this knowledge, the divine promises are clear in both aspects. If negativeness is sown in thought,

the same is produced and reaped. If positiveness is
sown in thought, then it is reaped. How then does one
turn the negative once sown and reap into the constructive?

This is done by the divine power in each of us, who
are Souls. The Shariyat-Ki-Sugmad, the ECK bible,
tells us, "Your life is hid with the ECK (the power) in
me." This is the divinely appointed bridge between
God and man, between good and evil, between positiveness and negativeness—enabling that which is
not good to become good, that which is unhappy to
become happy, and that which is incurable to become
curable.

The Chandogya Upanishad says, "That which is
infinite is bliss. In the finite there is no bliss. Infinitely alone is bliss. This infinity is to be realized. The
Self (Soul) is the infinite. Self is below, above, behind,
before, right and left; Self is all this.

"He who sees, perceives, understands, and loves
the Self, delights in the Self, revels in the Self, and
rejoices in the Self becomes the Lord and Master in
all the worlds."

Now you see that when one is the positive Self, the
state of the Soul, then the divine promises become
clear and it is seen that there is a perfect connection
between the statements that Jeremiah gave: "For thus
saith the Lord Thy bruise is incurable, and thy wound
is grievous," "Fear thou not. . . . I will save thee. . . . I
am with thee," and "I will restore health unto thee,
and I will heal thee of thy wounds."

Later he says, "Yea, I have loved thee with an
everlasting love: therefore with loving kindness have
I drawn thee."

The power of sowing and reaping has been given
to man because he is God's offspring and heir. He is

— *Jer 1:7*

free to sow and reap whatsoever he chooses; but always there is this divinely appointed "bridge" between the unknowing and the knowing, the human and divine. By this 'bridge' which is called the Mahanta, known to us as Divine Spirit, power, center, when we seek and unite with It, we are saved from the negativeness of sowing and come into a state of completion, of joy and of health.

Jeremiah was the great prophet of Israel and the son of Hilkiah, a high priest in the land of Benjamin. Before he came to earth the Lord gave Jeremiah the realization of the divine power, and appointed him as a prophet to serve the tribe of Israel.

Having the power of the Lord he was told, "Thou shalt go to all that I shall send you and whatsoever I command thee thou shalt speak." Jer. 1:7.

The Lord taught Jeremiah the hidden secret of knowledge. Truth is only for those who take the time and trouble to seek it out. He knew of the hidden side of God that has existed as a knowledge distinct from the science and philosophy of teachers who have written the Scriptures, or who have their master's words.

Why are those who know or possess this knowledge unwilling to let it pass into general circulation for the sake of betterment and success in struggling against deceit, evil, and ignorance?

Here is something that many of us have overlooked. This knowledge is not concealed from the eyes of the masses. The fact is that the enormous majority of people do not want knowledge; they refuse their share of it and do not take the rations allotted to them. *Do not want it*

Knowledge cannot belong to all, cannot even belong to many. This is the law. This is what the Lord tells Jeremiah, and for this reason alone it is evident that we find the savants counseling all to be humble when they receive the opportunity to know knowledge. Jesus kept repeating this: "I do nothing of myself," he declared. "The Father that dwelleth in me, He doeth the works. . . . He that believeth on me, the works that I do shall he do also." He made this emphatic.

Is there any truth so clear, so triumphant as this? And is it not truth that will stand the test of any happening on this earth?

Now in this world, this universe, knowledge like everything else is limited, because it is material. It is material in this universe for we are working with the two laws, the law of God and the law of man. That is why no single individual while in this universe can possess the whole of truth. Each generally knows something different about Truth than the other will know. For example: Bacon, Spinoza, Voltaire, Emerson, Berkeley, Kant, Hegel, Spencer, Schopenhauer, and Darwin contributed something to the knowledge of truth because the quality of matter in a given place and under given conditions is limited. This applies as well to divine knowledge and accounts for the fact that at certain periods of history, in certain centuries, there was a great amount of knowledge and a greater distribution of it, and that it even possessed different qualities than it does today.

If knowledge is distributed within a small group then it has a greater advantage than amongst larger numbers of people. It works on the same basis as currency, for if whatever one has in life is too small, it will change nothing for him. On the other hand, large quantities of knowledge will give great advantages. From this point of view, this knowledge sifting down from the higher regions makes it far more advantageous that knowledge be preserved among a smaller number of people and not dispersed among the masses.

Here on this Earth we are like the prodigal sons sent forth from our Father's House. We have forgotten who we are, what we are, and who and what our Father is. We have wandered along the byways and lost our way; we have fallen and hurt ourselves, damaging the lamp of intuition so that we no longer know why we are here. We have forgotten that God's blessings are always flowing, that we can contact them by becoming one with the same substance as the blessings. Oil and water do not mix. Neither do divine blessings and materiality of thought. We must become godlike in desire, for the more we desire of God, the more of God is given to us.

The truth is that the crowd neither wants nor seeks truth, and the leaders of the crowd, in their own interests, try to strengthen the mass fear and dislike of everything new and unknown. The slavery in which mankind lives is primarily based on this fear of the unknown, this resistance to change, even when it is obvious that the new is good.

There is no mystery about truth, but the acquisition and the transmission of true knowledge demands both great labor and great effort of him who receives.

Those who possess this knowledge are doing everything they can to transmit and communicate it to a striving and deserving number of people to facilitate their approach to it and enable them to prepare themselves to receive the truth.

Those who want truth must make the initial effort to find the source of knowledge and to approach it, taking advantage of the help and indications which are given to all, but which people as a rule do not want to see or recognize. Knowledge cannot come to you without effort on your part.

Strangely, most persons feel that truth can be

53

given them without much effort. However, this is a wrong attitude for great knowledge is not easy to gather to one's self. For example, it takes five to ten years to grasp the principles of medicine, and often the same or longer for the study of painting, writing, or music.

Many times an individual's independent effort will attain him nothing. It is usually gained through those who already possess it. One should learn from those who know.

Another of the great Biblical prophets, Isaiah, says, "So shall my word be that goeth forth out of my mouth: it shall not return unto me void, but it shall accomplish that which I please, and it shall prosper in the thing whereto I sent it."

Isaiah was speaking of the law of this particular world where life is a reflex of mental states. The character that things often bear will be the impress of our first conception of them. Whenever we place condemnation upon anything in life, it will strike back and hurt us. If we bless any situation, it has no power to hurt, and even if it is troublesome for a time it will gradually fade away—that is, if we bless it.

Now if we dwell upon the past or the probable future of the universe, the effort is generally useless. It is beyond our ken to predict generally with regard to the past or future world, plan for its reorganization and try to effect this, for this simply defeats one's own efforts. The best way to handle materiality is to begin to perceive the material universe as it is within the immediate present and examine what one sees at the moment of present time with the idea that one can encompass what one sees. Thus, fear of the material universe and what it contains simply diminishes and one moves again toward kingship.

An ancient sage, whose words have been recorded in the Kaushitaki Upanishad, says: "May my speech be established in thy mind. May my mind be fixed in thy speech O divine word. Thee spreads Thy powers through my words."

He was praising the power that all prophets say will help us, once contact is made with it. The power of self-knowledge is greater than any other power that exists anywhere in all the universes. Wherever there is life there is this ECK force existing, for life in itself is immortal and indestructible; it cannot change. Life in the abstract is always the same whether or not it is expressed outwardly. When we do not see the manifestation of life we say it is dead; but Life Force or God does not change, nor die. Very few people will understand the simplicity of this.

Indra, the Hindu God of the Angels, said, "I am Prana, know me as Prana, life. Worship me as the conscious Self, the source of intelligence." Prana is the Sanskrit word for the divine power. It is through this divine force that we attain immortality.

We must look upon this divine power existing in the universe as having two aspects: one, expressing itself as the Life Force; the other, as intelligence. They are inseparable from one another. Intelligence is that which is the source of consciousness.

The Life Force is the conscious Self. What is the Life Force? That which is self-conscious is the Life Force. We often call that which is conscious by the name of intelligence. We know that intelligence and activity in the ECK power is the Life Force within man. Activity and self-consciousness are inseparable and live together in the body; when together they leave it, the body is said to be dead.

When man dies, the ECK power takes with it the

same impressions and tendencies of the previous existence.

The Real Self is clothed with the Life Force, a portion of which manifests Itself subjectively as sense-power or subjects; similarly the subjects only exist as long as they are related to the objects.

A quick review of this is necessary. The ECK power, or Life Force, and self-consciousness are identical; the sense powers depend upon the Life Force, and objects are related to sensations because objects cannot exist independent of the powers of perception. The threads of sensation and sense power are woven from the forces of God power. The whole universe therefore depends on this ECK power, this self-consciousness. Self is the center of the universe as well as the center of each of us. It is the foundation of life, inseparable from the Life Force, and is the producer of all sense-power. Indeed, Self is the originator of the phenomenal universe.

ECK, Life Force, self-consciousness (whatever you wish to call It) is not many, for It is one. The Life Force in you is the same as the Life Force in me and in others. As Life Force is one, so self-consciousness is one. Self-consciousness exists as the root of all knowledge.

The man who succeeds, however great or small his aim, is he who refuses to be discouraged by discouragements, who refuses to give up when faced with disappointments, deadlocks, and delays. He is a part of the Supreme, and as that—the truth—he can do the impossible.

So many teachings seem to imply that the power can only be obtained through the intervention of another, that the power is within man but that it can only be contacted through stupendous or extraordinary means. Yet the fact is that the power is easily contacted by anyone who will believe this—so easily that the intellectual types often have difficulty in accepting this, while the more childlike leap on ahead of them.

Often people are surprised to learn that all power comes from within but they need to contact the Master, as they have been so often told to do. The ECK Masters tell us that the Spirit of truth will remain with us after they have left the earthly sight of man, and did they not add: "the ECK will lead you into all truth."

Fubbi Quantz gave us this promise of the Sugmad. "Blessed is that man that trusteth in the Supreme Being, for he shall be like the mighty banyan by the river that spreadeth out her roots; her leaves shall be green and shall bloom in the drought and blossom in the plentiful seasons."

What the ECK Master is telling us is that we can enter into the originating spirit of Life itself, and so reproduce it in ourselves as a perennial spring of living. We, ourselves, are the living embodiment of truth. Consequently, the direction taken by our creative and positive action is never dictated by outward circumstances, and the primary movement is, therefore, entirely due to the action of the Spirit of God within ourselves outflowing into the action of manifestation in the outer world.

Furthermore, this spiritual action is purely a matter of feeling. It is what we speak of as motif in a work of art, literature, or music. So you see, a very high purpose in the universe is the creation of an effect. One creates effect through thought, feeling, and action.

It is this original feeling that we need to enter into, because it is the origin of the whole chain of causation which subsequently follows. What can this original feeling of the Spirit be? Since the Life Force is life-in-itself, Its feeling is for the fuller expression of life; any other feeling would be self-destructive and therefore inconceivable.

The full expression of life implies happiness; happiness implies harmony and harmony implies order; order implies proportion and proportion implies beauty. So in recognizing the inherent tendency of the Spirit to produce life, we recognize a similar inherent tendency toward the other qualities mentioned. The desire to bestow the fullness of joyous life can be described as love; thus we can sum up the whole of the feeling, which is the original moving impulse of the Spirit, as love and beauty.

Spirit finds expression through forms of beauty in centers of life, in harmonious reciprocal relations to Itself.

Divine truth is one and unchanging. Desire truth and you will then find the inner meaning unfolding. Everything has its origin in Spirit. One decides to invent a machine. He first creates it in thought, believing in its power to do a certain work. Then he takes the necessary steps to bring it into visible being. We ask and believe and give something mental existence. The necessary steps are unfolded from within to bring it into visible being. So you see, a Master states divine truth, when he says we must ask and believe, to have. Unless we first give a thing mental existence it can never have physical existence.

Look at it like this, especially if you are having difficulty with visualization. No one can look closely with the mind's eye. It is more a relaxed and easy sensing of the object. The inward vision does not work in the same way as our outer vision. It goes more keenly into the object, seeing more, but with less strain.

Do not be in too much of a hurry for it may take time. Whenever difficulties of visualization come to your mind, say firmly to yourself, "I can visualize a little already, so I have only to develop what I already know." Everyone visualizes unknowingly when looking forward to something. Until you can visualize to your entire satisfaction, think and feel consciously, all the while practicing visualization.

Yaubl Sacabi, the great ECK Master, says: "There are three basic truths. They are: One—We are the offspring and heirs of God. Therefore we inherit the power to mold the God power by the thoughts we think. Two—What we think, if held to, comes to pass in our lives. Thus we learn by experience. Three—Through learning by experience, we become conscious children of God, and presently come into the glorious liberty of the children of God."

One cannot really explain spiritual consciousness to people who have not attained it. Those who have not attained it look at the Living ECK Master for his physical attributes. It is like the antics of children. They immediately link him with their consciousness of his appearance, and he is no longer able to cooperate without restraint from the inward heights of spiritual love. He becomes to them like a social worker, living an outer life in the world.

You should never question, but only desire to live in closeness with the Supreme Spirit. Then you will receive the fullness of Truth, Wisdom, and Spiritual love. The fruits of the spiritual consciousness become your own property.

Now without the element of individual personality the Spirit, or Soul, can only work cosmically by a generic law; it must work solely with plants or minerals, that state of being which has only the lowest consciousness. The law of God is a far higher specialization, and this specialization can only be attained through the introduction of the personal factor.

However, if the individual desires to produce this factor within himself, he must be fully aware of the principle which underlies the spontaneous, cosmic action of the law of God. Where, then, will he find this principle of life? Certainly not by contemplating death.

I find that to get a principle to work in the way I require, I must observe its action when it is working spontaneously in this particular direction. I ask myself why it goes in the right direction as far as it does, and having learned this I am able to make it go further.

The knowledge of a principle is to be gained by the study of its affirmative action. When I have understood this, I am in a position to correct any negative conditions which tend to prevent that action.

So you see, the prophet Jeremiah was great not because he told the people of Israel that God would do something for them if they lived up to the divine law, but because he showed what would happen if they failed to do so.

In cooperation with the law, it is as Rebazar Tarzs, the ECK Master, states, "We become Co-workers with God!"

Jeremiah points out, "Am I a God at hand, saith the Lord, and not a God afar off? Can any hide himself in secret places that I shall not see him? Do I not fill heaven and earth? saith the Lord."

ECK, the Life Force, is within you and me. Death is the absence of consciousness, of awareness, and disease is the absence of health. To enter into the

60

spirit of Life we are required to contemplate it where it is.

God is found to be working through untold ages, not merely as deathless energy, but as a perpetual advance into higher degrees of consciousness. If we could only encompass the Spirit, so as to make it evident in ourselves, as it is, in itself, the greater work, the magnum opus would be accomplished. This simply means a realization of our spiritual life, as drawn directly from the divine power. Now we can understand that thought, the imagination of the Spirit, is the greater reality of being, and that all outer situations, objects, and circumstances are only correspondences that are the result of our thought pictures. All we have to do is to maintain our individual place in the divine power.

I have learned that man is not part of the great generic pattern which molds all forms, nor of any particular circumstances, but is a separate creation existing in the absolute ideal.

I know that we must learn to disassociate ourselves from particular circumstances, and to rest upon our absolute nature, as the reflection of the divine ideal. We in turn reflect back to the power of God its original conception of itself as expressed in the typical man. Thus, by the Law of Cause and Effect those who realize this mental attitude enter permanently into the Spirit of Divine Power, and It becomes a perennial fountain of life springing up spontaneously within themselves.

I find in myself as the ECK teachings say, "the image and likeness of God." I have reached the level for a new starting point for creative action, and the divine power finding a personal center in me, has started its work anew. I have solved the problem that enables the Spirit or divine Self to act directly upon this plane in particular, or in any other plane.

Each of us is a microcosm, a universe in miniature, and we are the requisite center for a new entrance of creative spirit.

How can I convince anyone that to find the ECK power for use in life is easy?

Jesus said, "Except that ye be converted and become as little children, ye shall not enter into the kingdom of heaven." And again, "The kingdom of God is within you." Also, he said lovingly, "Come ye yourselves apart into a desert place, and rest a while." Thus, I, of the Mahanta Consciousness, tell you this: By resting in the ECK power, surrendering to It as little children, you may gain both wisdom and strength. They come through your inward resting, relaxing, in the knowledge that all is being taken care of by the divine power of the living God.

Remember, John the Baptist said, "Repent ye: for the kingdom of heaven is at hand." This can affirm your faith for it means for you to change your thinking from outward to inward for the kingdom of heaven can only be contacted by seeking the Kingdom of God within.

 We must not seek the solution to our problems from the outer. We must have faith in our ability to use the God State that is within us, which we have been using constantly all our lives. Have you not experienced this state at times when everything has come your way and you felt at ease with all? This suggests trust in God.

If you want to express yourself or do anything intensely enough; dream it, imagine it and believe in it, and you will make contact with the ECK power and it will be so. It is the inner with which you make contact. In this way you become magnetized with your faith, and then you are drawn into the situations and circumstances that you are longing for.

Our creed should be, "I believe." How can one become any simpler in his language than this? It gives the widest scope to the experience of regeneration by relaxing, by letting go (at least psychologically) of the tension held to the breast. It is the acceptance of the grace of the ECK Life Force that comes pouring in to rebuild the body, and keep it youthful, poised and ready for emergencies. It is giving the body and mind direction and letting the Real Self, Soul, express.

Spirit has a single motivation, a primary impulse, which is to express truth, the love and beauty it feels itself to be. Thus, I know that the essence of Spirit is nobility, aesthetics, life, love, and beauty. It cannot act in any particular circumstance except by becoming the particular, nor can it act upon any material or other plane object except by expression through itself, and every individual.

Individuality is the necessary complement of the Spirit. The whole problem of life consists of finding the true relationship of self, the individual, to the true power, to the true Spirit. So the first step is to realize what this power must be in Itself.

If Spirit is a law unto itself to express life, love, and beauty, then the answer is found in man's consciousness. I cannot be conscious of anything except by realizing a certain relationship between it and myself. I must have it affect me in some way, otherwise I am not conscious of its existence. According to the way it affects me, I recognize myself as being related to it. It is this self-recognition on my part with all the relationships I establish, whether spiritual, intellectual, or physical, that constitutes my realization of life. This is the principle for the realization of living and the creation of centers of life. Through this action conscious realization can be attained and divine power flows through me.

No true realization of Spirit can take place in you unless you are free to accept it or reject it. An example of this is love; love must be spontaneous or it has no existence. There is no such thing as mechanically induced love. Anything which is formed so that it automatically produces an effect, without any volition of its own, is nothing but a machine.

If the Spirit is to realize the reality of love, it must be in relation to some individual who has the power to give or withhold love. In other words, you must have perfect freedom to love or not to love, otherwise you will suffer the flow-back of energy which ordinarily causes an adverse effect upon yourself. This also applies to any quality of life, any circumstance in this physical world or other planes.

So it is in proportion, that I, the Real Self, an independent center of action, with the option of acting either positively or negatively, produce any real life. The further the created thing is from being a crude mechanical arrangement, the higher is the quality of creation. The solar system is a high mechanical creation, the expression of law as laid down by a number of planetary spirits, who directed it into being. However, it keeps its motion due to the supervision of planetary spirits who keep it moving on course using the highest nature of the ECK power.

Spirit does not require a mechanism, however perfect. It is Soul described as "man made in the image of God," and is, in itself, an independent source of action. Spirit is far more than a mechanical device.

Earlier I said that divine knowledge was limited.

It is for this reason that the life, love, and beauty of God are not visibly reproduced in every person. These qualities are pseudoproduced in the worlds, including the physical universe, as far as mechanical and automatic action can represent them, but because too many Souls have lost their responsibility toward themselves, they go no further than mechanical creations. These, oftentimes, are accepted as the real thing.

The full creation of the qualities of spirit, life, love, and beauty can only take place on the basis of a freedom akin to that of the ECK power Itself which implies a total freedom from negation as well as from positiveness.

Why, even so, would an individual make a negative choice? It is because he does not understand the law of his own individuality and believes it to be a law of limitation, instead of a law of liberty. He does not expect to find the starting point of a creative activity reproduced within himself, and so looks to the mechanical side of things for the basic fundamentals of life.

Following this same reasoning he is led to the conclusion that life is limited. He has assumed limitation in his premises and logically he cannot escape from its inevitable conclusion.

Because he thinks this is the law, he ridicules the idea of transcending it. He believes in the sequence of cause and effect by which death, disease, and disaster hold sway over him and others, and he says this sequence is law. He is right so far as he goes for it is a law. But not *the* law. He has made it a law for himself. He has accepted a law of others, which, if not exactly the same, has the same result.

Lai Tsi, who gave the masses the Word of God, spoke of dire consequences. Through Lai Tsi, God was telling the Chinese in his day what would happen should they follow the path of the lower self. Lai Tsi made promises to the people that if they properly used their freedom of choice, they could have the treasures of heaven.

These principles show us the place which is occupied by the personal consciousness of the individual. They lead us to an intelligence which is beyond the present limited manifestation of the spiritual law.

Manifested, they constitute the instrumentality by which the infinite possibilities of Spirit can be evoked into forms of power, usefulness, and beauty.

5

Behold the Wisdom

In anyone's search for truth there are always found many pundits, sannyasins, sadhus, maulawiyahs, and savants, who have proclaimed to know the secret knowledge of the Spirit. But the majority of them are not aware of the real wisdom of God. You must investigate them and if they are found wanting, turn away and seek those who understand the real teachings of the ECK power; seek those who will show you the techniques for achievement by the Real Self, and the practices to avoid in order to save oneself from the snares of the mind, of maya and of illusion.

Any teacher who gives forth as a system the spiritual practice of having their initiates concentrate their attention on the muladhara chakra or ganglion, which is called in western physiology the coccyx nerve center at the base of the spine, and upward along the spine to the Spiritual Eye, is simply wasting time and effort. Even with great labor and much loss of time very few ever reach the Spiritual Eye.

The Spiritual Eye is represented as the pineal gland. From the divine essence through the Spiritual Eye come many teachings. In the system of ECK Masters, concentration is begun at this eye until one

is ready to project from the body. All of the lower
centers are disregarded. They are body centers and
have existence as the body consciousness and are
concerned with the lower self.

During the sixth century B.C., when I studied under
the great Pythagoras of Greece, I learned that he was
concerned mainly with two points in the teaching of
truth. First, an emphasis of love, wisdom, and charity,
and secondly, that the kingdom of heaven was within
man.

These two precepts are cardinal points in the teachings of the saints. Pythagoras's greatest statement
was, "So that, ascending into the radiant Ether, midst
the Immortals, shall be thyself a God."

This was the basic point of his teachings. It dis-
turbed the establishment of his day so much that after
his death in 500 B.C., the masses were incited to attack
and destroy Pythgoras's followers and schools at
Crotona and Metapontum. Fortunately I escaped both
disasters including the fate of those who were compelled to die of thirst and hunger in the Temple of the
Muses.

This singular statement by Pythagoras later became the credo for those initiates and adepts who
followed the path established by this remarkable man.
He emphasized that it is required to get the principles
of ECK power affirmatively working under higher
conditions than those spontaneously present in man.
This was to be done by the introduction of the personal
element, an individual intelligence capable of compre-
hending the principle.

What is the principle by which we came into being?
It is simply the originating movement of Soul that
takes place in the divine power. This is analogous to
picturing in mind, what we might call imaginative

prototypes. I, the individual, as the microcosm, am capable of reproducing all the qualities of the Sugmad. Consequently, I have learned that I, as Soul, the seeming product of this Sugmad am imaging forth an image of myself on this physical world plane which is the direct image of that in other planes.

The control center is Soul, the "I," the cause factor in man. It directs through the emotional relay systems, the actions of the body and the environment. The function of "I," Soul, is judgment, the estimation of what effort is required to do something.

This is the deep secret of the mysteries of the Vairagi, the ancient order of the ECK Masters. Pythagoras was one of the first who was well versed in the "mysteries of what effort is required to do something." He knew it was useless for the initiate to concentrate on the chakras, the body spine centers, except for disciplinary exercise. Concentration on body centers does not lead to control of the body and environment.

According to Pythagoras, Soul could be at one of three points in relation to the body. It could be inside the head, just outside the skull, or off at a distance.

The great Greek Master says that it is known among the wise ones that the top of the head is the point at which the human merges with the ECK Spirit. Very young children have a soft spot on the head where the opening has not quite closed, and one has only to observe the eyes and expression of a very young child to know that he or she is in closer contact with the Divine than adults.

As the spot closes, the child grows more worldly in outlook and expression.

Those who wish to be initiated into the consciousness of the Divine, that of the Inner Kingdom, must become as little children. The opening must remain in the top of the head, like that soft spot of the infant. This can be achieved in the spiritual counter body, so it need not be developed in the physical. Yet despite this fact, ECK Masters do keep the spot open deliberately by the use of certain spiritual exercises. The Tibetan saint Milarepa practiced this and asked all his disciples to do likewise—as does Rebazar Tarzs.

This opening at the top of the head is symbolized in the phrase "Narrow Way," which is the name given to the small insignificant and closely guarded door at the entrance where the Spirit enters and leaves the body. Jesus referred to this spot in the head when he said: "Strait is the gate, and narrow is the way, which leadeth unto life, and few there be that find it." He spoke both of the narrow way of the initiation chamber and the narrow way that had to be opened, and kept open at the top of the head, as with a little child. He spoke of this often when saying to his followers, "Except ye be converted and become as little children, ye shall not enter into the kingdom of heaven."

The narrow way, the soft spot opening at the top of the head, is the meeting place of Soul with the body. It is through this opening that spiritual awareness (God or cosmic consciousness) occurs. Do you remember the story of Balaam and the ass in the book of Numbers? The ass symbolizes the physical opening in the top of the head and Balaam the spiritual opening. The ass saw an angel standing in the way, in a narrow place, but Balaam could not see the angel. Then God, the Spiritual Awareness, entered into Soul opening and Balaam saw the angel there. After that he had the power to speak only in the highest truth. He was, in fact, initiated and aware of the divine power and the use of it.

The ECK Masters know this secret. It has rarely been written about clearly. Instead only the vaguest references have been made concerning it here and there. To preserve this secret the men of the East chose young children whose parents wished to give them to God for a life of service as candidates for initiation. By special exercises they kept the soft spot open until the Soul became set in its opening. Our own christening ceremony was originally for this purpose, but long ago the true reason was lost and forgotten and so its power has gone. The christening or water ceremony was to make a person as though "born again," and the confirmation ceremony was to confirm or set the opening in both the physical and Soul bodies, thus enabling the initiate to enter the Christ Consciousness within while still on earth. This is the true meaning of those words, so little understood today. "Except a man be born again. . . . Except a man be born of water and of the Spirit, he cannot enter the kingdom of God."

The aperture which you can visualize as opening above you, into direct contact with the divine power, is the opening at the top of the head which will indeed open gradually, in Soul. This is your first ceremony as a candidate for initiation, and its constant use will enable you to become fully initiated in time to be as born again, as ascending into the midst of the immortals and thyself becoming a God. Here is the secret of the wonderful happiness and freedom from care experienced by so many who follow the science of the Divine Spirit; the secret of their closeness to God, of a quickly growing faith that brings them closer to their heart's desire.

If we go to Soul, the real "I" in ourselves, which philosophy and scriptures declare to be made in the image and likeness of God, we have reached that which

71

stands supreme above the outer vehicles. It creates all outerness, for it occupies the place of first cause. On the other hand this must not lead us into thinking there is nothing higher; for Soul is the effect of an antecedent cause which we call Oversoul, the divine essence.

We find ourselves holding an intermediate position between true first cause on the one hand, and the world of secondary causes on the other. In order to understand the nature of this position we must study and reach the understanding that divine power can work only in this physical world plane in its particular manner through the individual. Then we see that the function of the individual is to differentiate and distribute all flows of power in suitable directions for starting the various trains of secondary causation.

I have found that man's place in the cosmic order is that of a distributor of divine power, subject to the inherent law of the power he distributes. We never create force; all we do is distribute it. For this reason man is spoken of in the scriptures as a steward or dispenser of divine gifts. As our minds become open to the full meaning of this position, the immense possibilities and the resultant responsibility contained therein will become apparent.

The individual, the Soul, is the creative center of his own world. We must accept this as a part of the responsibility of life. The true nature of man is always present, only we have in the past taken the lower and mechanical side of things for our starting point. So we have created limitations instead of expansion.

However, even with the divine knowledge of creative cycles we shall continue to restrict if we seek our starting point in things below us instead of in the divine power. Life is being. It is the experience of

72

states of consciousness and there is an unfailing similarity between these inner states and the outward conditions. So you see, it is from the original creation, in divine power, that the state of consciousness must be the cause, and the similar conditions the effect. The reason the corresponding conditions are an effect is because at the starting of the creation no conditions existed, the actual working of the Sugmad, the ECK power, upon itself can only have been a state of consciousness. The creative order moves from states to conditions; man has inverted this order and sought to create from conditions to states. Seldom do conditions create the desired state.

If neither of these ways is understood, one should make mental self-recognition the starting point, knowing that by the inherent law of Spirit, the correlated conditions will come by a natural process. We must realize that self-recognition is that of our relation to Spirit, the generating center, with the individual as the distributing center. This is similar to electricity which is generated at the central station and delivered in different forms by reason of passing through appropriate centers of distribution. In one place it lights a room, in another conveys a message, and in a third drives a train; in like manner the power that Spirit becomes is a particular form through an individual Soul. It does not interfere with the lines of his individuality, but works along them, thus making him not less, but more himself. It is, thus, not a compelling force, but an expanding and illuminating power. The more one recognizes the reciprocal action between the power and himself, the more full his life must become.

One should not be troubled about future conditions because the power of Spirit is working through each of us and for each of us, and that, according to the law, produces all the conditions required for the expression of life, love and beauty. So we can fully trust it to open the way as we go along in life. Take no thought, which means do not worry, or have anxious thoughts. This is a practical application of sound philosophy. Of course, we must exert ourselves. I must do my share in the work and not expect God to do for me what It can do only through me. We must use our natural faculties in working on the conditions now present, and make use of them as far as they go. But we must not try to go further than what the present requires. It is not necessary to force issues. Allow them to grow naturally, knowing that they are doing so under the guidance of Spirit.

We should develop the habit of looking at our mental attitude as the key to progress in life, knowing that everything else must come out of it. We shall further discover that our mental attitude is eventually determined by the way in which we regard the divine power. The final result will be that we shall see the power of Spirit to be identical with life, love, and beauty. These in turn being identical with wisdom and the perfect adjustments of parts to the whole. We will learn to see ourselves as distributing centers of these primary energies and as subordinate centers of creative power. The automatically responding self is then the partial expression, and the goal is nothing less than freedom. Not freedom without law but freedom according to the law. We become like God when we see It as It is, because this whole process, individualizing in man, is a reflection of the primal image existing in Divine Spirit.

For this very reason one should realize more perfectly the relation between the individual and Spirit, as one of reciprocal action. If you grasp this fact of reciprocity, you will then understand why some persons fall short of expressing the fullness of life, which Spirit is, and why others attain the fullness. It is the same principle by which iron will usually sink in water but can be made to float. It is the individualizing of Divine Spirit, by its reciprocity of action that alone is the secret of the perpetuation and growth of one's individuality.

To understand the importance that attitude assumes in our efforts to survive as a physical being, and more basically as a spiritual being, let us examine a scale which we will lay out in the following sentences. Any similarity to other scales is coincidental and immaterial. It is understanding we wish here, not the slavish following of a scale.

Studying the many and varied philosophies and systems one finds the following scale extant and so fully elaborated in many cases that we have come to agree upon its form.

Like any system of measurement, you arrive at your conclusions through observations. As you examine the apparent inner emotional life and the outer behavior you can find a correlating position on this scale of attitudes and so find the personal survival factor of that moment under conditions prevalent at that moment. You will, in fact, find, as you begin to experiment, an entire gamut of emotional responses dramatized by the inner self corresponding to these various positions on this scale.

You will find that when a person recalls a very painful incident, he drops into blackness, an unawareness, an unconsciousness, and sometimes apparent death. As the incident is reexperienced, he often shows apathy. Through successive reexperiencing, he may dramatize grief, fear, hidden hostility, anger, antagonism, boredom, conservatism, exhilaration, enthusiasm, and serenity. This succession of emotions carefully observed can be finally established in one's mind.

As a person descends below what we might call the death point, or total unawareness of what is going on around him, one finds states of unconsciousness in varying degrees. Above this is pretended death and the state known in psychology as catatonia. Above this is the attitude of making amends, then changing followed by grief, propitiation, sympathy, shame, blame, and regret. As one goes up toward the whole, as toward the God State, he would enter into covert hostility and anger in varying degrees, followed by the complete expression of antagonism. It is in this state that we find a dividing line between health and sickness. Below it the person is increasing his attempts to succumb. Above anger, he is attempting to survive and is surviving in increasing measure.

As a person goes below the anger band, he becomes increasingly weaker and succumbs more than he survives. This does not necessarily include an acute temporary state but refers more to chronic states of grief, anger, and apathy. The closer to death a person is, the more predictable he becomes. A dead body is very predictable, and a person who is pretending death is somewhat less predictable. Grief, hidden hostility, and anger are states which have very definite characteristics and make those at this level more set in their ways.

A person who is consistently at a given level has certain habits, behavior and physical characteristics, i.e., one at chronic anger will try to hold or stop motion. For example a parent who wishes to make a child stop an activity will use anger in doing so. The chronically angry person tends to have depository illnesses such

as arthritis. He likes to talk about death and destruction and is primarily interested in communication
concerning these. He will attempt to destroy opposing
realities by stating they are wrong and violently dis-
agreeing with the reality of others. He tends to use sex
as punishment and his treatment of children is often
brutal. His ethical level is poor and destructive and
he will be actively dishonest. He will be guilty of
blatant and destructive lying, and what bravery he
has will be damaging to himself. He will assume
responsibilities in order to destroy, and has little
persistence. His sense of humor is brutal, and he uses
threats, punishment, and alarming lies to dominate
other people. He considers present time bad and himself very important indeed. This set of characteristics
can be observed in a person who is in acute or chronic
anger.

Much can be said about this part of the spiritual
knowledge, but this is only a sample, and from there
we go to the point of faith; of having faith in one's self.
It is normal for people to have faith in a power greater
than themselves. Even savages have this and set up
a symbol of this power in the shape of a tree, an
animal, a bundle of feathers or a carving on a rock.
People who have no faith are really afraid to let themselves go. They hold rigidly to what they can see of
themselves and set themselves up as little gods. No
one who has faith in the limited, temporal body can
possibly be stronger than one who has faith in the
eternal, ever-present all-knowingness of God. So the
one with faith goes quietly along. Frequently the ones
who are scornful will be speechless, anyway, because
of the results of a practical faith.

There are two ways of meeting the difficulties of
the present or those that creep up from the past to

Blessings

bother us. (1) To view them, either in memory or present appearance as a battering ram, and to fall over backward and be flattened to the ground. (2) To view them as vital, valuable lessons which will educate and lift up—to view them as a springboard which will give the necessary incentive and energy to climb up and out.

This brings me to a point made long ago that I would never live up to the measure of what people think or what people say. I would always live according to my own conscience and take whatever was to come with it. Therefore, I arrange my life to make it easy. Frankly, I enjoy the leisure which enables me to feel aloof from human ties yet with humanity. So, instead of placing confidence in myself, it is placed in God. Its Spirit actually lives in all men. God knows everyone so that there is no need to test any person, but life does give one an opportunity to test himself. Faith is based upon the exact knowledge of God, Its love, justice, and perfection. If I have faith in God, this sure knowledge remains unwavering and unshakable, despite whatever comes into my life.

It comes to mind there was the ancient commandment "Thou shalt have no other gods before me." Most people imagine this was given because God wanted all praise for Itself. But a moment's reflection would tell anyone that this is not possibly true. It is the reflection of a perfect, all loving God. Whatever God wills or fulfills, Its purpose is for the benefit of man; that man may develop spiritually, unfold his inner self, enjoy perfect joy, health, and peace and come into the freedom of the Princes of God. Once we realize this, we can become co-workers of God, we can sing "Thy will be done, O God; O mighty Spirit of Love!"

Many have fallen out of tune with Its spirit of

joyfulness. They have found one thing in common, however varied their life may be. The other god they have chosen has been emotion, allowing it to assume supremacy over all other things, instead of taking its proper place. This god of emotion, if broken down, can warp judgment, destroy self-control, make fools of men, make them selfish and unheeding of the welfare of others. It makes them love that which is unlovable and causes disharmony with the natural flow of Spirit. They become spiritual misfits.

Emotion leads one away from the consciousness of the real self and centers on the outer circumstance; weakens the attention given previously to the "I"; influences others against their will to exercise reluctant choices or to live in sensations. An old saying is apt here, "Thou wilt keep him in perfect peace, whose mind is stayed on thee!"

The force of personal faith, enthusiasm and love are prime forces that make up the wisdom of God. We can find it when we "Behold the Wisdom" of the great and use the lives of the saints as our examples, and see behind the words that come out of their mouths.

6

The Unknown Name of God

*I*n the days before I became dissatisfied with the overgeneralized statements of those supposedly in the know, I read, researched, and listened to anyone who described the divine knowledge. While I have not associated myself with any of the above in years, I rather imagine they are still running rampant trying to put their ideas into circulation and causing confusion among the populace about love, wisdom, and God.

Most of the nonessentials of divine wisdom were invented or were openly promoted when Truth was forced to go underground due to persecution by church and state. These two groups did not wish for men to learn lest they observe ways and means of bettering their downtrodden condition and try to overthrow the established orders. The saviors did not have the worldwide means of instantaneous communication which we have today, and could not reach enough people to make their teachings effective enough to have lasting strength except for a few, like Christ and Buddha. So what we got as holy scriptures was little more than a pale reflection of truth. In many cases, it makes me wonder what is actually hidden in the hearts of many who know, but who will not tell the truth to the masses of people. It has been every man for himself, and much truth has been hidden behind symbolism in the writings of the Magi and wise men of the ages. A lot of guesswork by self-styled savants has been born and written for the public. Students of truth have been compelled to seek truth the best way possible, through records left, through researching among those living who have claimed to know and whose words have had to be tested. A lot of unsound guesswork has been made. Today all seekers have inherited the job of sifting out the useless and trying to rediscover what has been hidden or lost. It is a gargantuan task, and there are few authentic teachers and centers among the thousands of utterly useless promulgators of shallow doctrine.

The experiences of the seekers lead them into realizing that something is beyond the sweetness and light of the leaders they may have been following. Mainly, this comes about for the simple reason that what they have been hearing and reading did not have agreement. Contradictions started them looking deeper into the subject and into their own experiences to find truth. Many learned that they couldn't share their newly hard-won knowledge because of the possible dangerous aspects of spreading truth.

Once the individual becomes emancipated from the conventions of society he can easily become a criminal in the eyes of that society. Few really want change, peculiarly enough. Few understand that truth reveals itself only to those who seek it and love it. The whole purpose of spiritual training is, therefore, the absolute union with the Divine Self.

Buddha said, "The summit of Reality can only be realized within oneself." Schopenhauer stated, "The essential to life's happiness resides in what one has in one's Self." The principal source of human life comes from within and from the depth of the Soul. The jewels of the ECK wisdom are seldom strewn along the highway for people, but are left to the individual to find and know. The masses are never lifted to the position of understanding, nor have the religionists ever wanted them to be. It would mean lost trade for the pseudo-mystics.

Yet many true seekers have found something. At least I found through experience that the Giani Marg, the path of wisdom, is simple once it is found. Hazrat Inayat Khan gave me the clue in his writings, "He who depends on his eyes for sight, his ears for hearing and his mouth for speech, is still dead."

I found that the ECK teachings were completely intact in their lineage throughout the centuries. I soon learned that the science of the ECK knowledge could not be taught, but rather caught; and once caught, one never had to be in physical association with the higher beings, or teachings, again. I have had association with them and all teachings anywhere and everywhere in all worlds, on all planets, with all beings regardless of where they might be.

It is said that the Magi, the wise men of the East, were part of the ECK movement. As far as I can understand, Zarathustra, the Persian sage who lived hundreds of years B.C., was one of the Masters of the Ancient Order of the Vairagi, to which all ECK Masters belong. It actually came into being after the departure of the teacher, by a group of his followers who formed what came to be known as the Magi.

The secret and unknown name of God was first given light by the ECK Masters—that which we call HU, the beginning and ending of all.

The Supreme has been called various names in different languages, but it is known to those who recognize the real wisdom as HU, the name of the nameless one. The word *HU* is the Spirit of all sounds and of all words, and is hidden under them all as the Spirit of Soul. It does not belong to any language; no language can help belonging to it. This alone is the true name of God, a name that no people and no religion can claim as their own. This word is not only uttered by human beings but it is repeated by animals and birds. All things and beings exclaim this name of the Lord, for every activity of life expresses distinctly this very sound. This is the word mentioned in the Bible as existing before light came into this world: "In the beginning was the Word, and the Word was with God, and the Word was God."

In English, the word *human* explains two facts which are characteristic of humanity—HU means God, and man means mind. In other words, HU, God, is in all things and all beings, but it is only man by whom It is known, who is capable of knowing Me. Human, therefore, means God-Conscious being, God-Realized, or the God-Man. There are many corruptions of the word *HU* found in the Bible—Eloi, Elohim and Alleluia which came from the original word *HU*.

The word, the avenue of Spirit, is the real liberation for anyone. The word *HU* was the first manifestation of the Divine Creator, and the rest of creation, including the ethers and other elements, were created by the sound of HU. The Spirit current, HU, was the prime mover and the first impulse that came from the Deity and also the first cause of motion, color and form.

The vibratory motion of the word is confined to the spheres where matter exists in subtle, pure, less pure, and coarse form. A simpler explanation is that it is the manifestation of an effort on the part of HU, descending from the highest plane, to remove the carnal coating of the word in the lower planes.

It is known clearly that instead of Sound being the result of vibratory motion, It is really the prime mover of all in the infinite planes as well as vibratory motion, which again is instrumental in furthering the worlds of creation in the material planes.

In the physical universe sound currents originate from vibratory motion and have the purpose of carrying on the work of creation in various ways. The original word current, HU, is the father of all motions, forces, lights, sounds, and elements that subsequently came into existence in the Fifth Plane and belong to It.

The Spirit rays, or Souls, are residing in HU's continuum of forms throughout all planes and in all times. They exist in bodies to form the creation of various spheres in space giving them the power of motion through reason or life. The whole creation extending from the highest to the lowest sphere is sustained by Spirit rays, by Souls from God, and disappears or is dissolved on the separation of Spirit from the coatings, the bodies in which It resides.

The whole creation which man, plant, creature, or mineral feels, sees, and observes owes its origin and growth to the Word, or the ECK Spirit, is sustained throughout by ECK, and disappears or is dissolved when ECK is separated or withdrawn from the manifestation.

To approach the originating ECK, what is called the Father, man must first approach and catch Its ray, its ECK current, and then follow and trace Its course to God. Man must first know himself and then know HU, the source of the ECK Current, the Almighty Father, lying within the microcosm that man is.

The ECK Current and Its agent currents are flowing downward and outward toward the physical universe objects. To approach the center, man must change
the direction of the current upward or inward toward
the eternal source. This means giving up certain desires
in order to proceed on the journey to your self—you, the
individual "I."

Scientists say that matter and motion are the
principal factors in creation. This may be true so far
as the physical universe is concerned. But they do not
nor cannot say how or whence these two factors origi-
nated. Motion needs a sponsor and this sponsor is the
same Spirit, the word issuing forth like rays of the sun
from various centers, from spiritual-material suns,
diffused over all space comprising the physical universe system.

The energy atom is in itself a ray or current issuing
forth from a center atom and is endowed with Spirit
power which is called energy by the scientists.
Unmanifested power is called latent, potential energy
and that which is apparently expressed—kinetic energy. Both aspects apply to the impulses from the ECK
force which is the origin and beginning of all.

Atoms play their part in our solar system; for
example, they issue forth from the Sun. As suns above
the worlds, they are manifested sun orbs before they
are issued forth as rays or currents and are thus fitted
for the work of creation of parts of the bodies they
combine to form and to which they give existence. The
ECK Current, latent in these atoms, is steeped in the
matter of the lower spheres, and It requires an impulse from a higher current or word, especially HU,
appertaining to and descending from the higher sphere,
to awaken Its energy and move It into action.

Thus, you see, ECK power or force is all, in all, the

principal factor, the prime action in the whole creation. It is the life and Soul of everything.

I have endeavored to reach some conception of the unknown name of God, what It is in Itself, and of the relation of the individual to It. So far as we can form any conception of these things at all, we see that they are universal principles applicable to all nature, and at the human level applicable to all men. They are general laws, the recognition of which is an essential preliminary to any further advance, because progress is made, not by setting aside the inherent law of things, which is impossible, but by specializing it, through presenting conditions which will enable the same principle to act in a less limited manner. Having, therefore, gotten a general idea of these two ultimates, the universal and the individual, and of their relation to one another, let us now consider the process of specialization. In what does the specialization of this HU consist? It consists in making that law or principle produce an effect which it could not produce under the simple generic conditions spontaneously provided by nature.

The Holy Spirit, ECK, divine power all mean exactly the same thing. In the New Testament, Jesus clearly mentions actually hearing the sound of HU, the Spirit, which can give new birth. He says, "The wind bloweth where it listeth (wishes), and thou hearest the sound thereof, but canst not tell whence it cometh, and whither it goeth."

Now to go on with this point. The selection of suitable conditions is the work of intelligence, it is a process of consciously arranging things in a new order, so as to produce new results. The principle of HU is never new for its principles are eternal and universal, but the knowledge that the same principle will produce

87

unfoldment of infinite possibilities is a startling statement. Therefore, we must even watch our speech and
words. It was Apollonius of Tyana who once said, "Soul
is surrounded by enemies. No one, nothing, is Its friend.
Even the mind watches It like a cat regards a rat as
something to be eaten. Even those Spirits who are
votaries of Rawhan (evil) and obey its laws, that is, the
dictates of the mind, suffer this pain. All are subject
to pain, so long as they are in this realm of earth and
things."

What we have to consider is the working of the
power in providing specific conditions, through our
actions and choices, for the operation of universal
principles. This is to bring about new results which
will transcend our past experiences. The process does
not consist in the introduction of new elements, but
in making new combinations of elements which are
always present. For example, our forefathers had no
conception of the elements of chemistry which have
always been in existence.

Then how are we to bring the power of HU to bear
upon the physical laws relating to the individual and
cosmic Spirit to enhance our understanding of these
laws and to produce greater results than those which
we have hitherto obtained?

It is done by always inquiring as to what is the
affirmative, the positive factor in any existing combination, and asking ourselves why this is so in this
particular combination? Why does it not act beyond
certain limits? What makes a thing a success, insofar
as it goes, and what prevents it going further?

Now we are coming to the method of creation.
What is the first positive factor in the whole creation?
As we look at it, this factor is Spirit—the invisible
power which concentrates the primordial ether into

forms and endows those forms with various modes of motion, from the simply mechanical motion of the planets to volitional motion in man. So then, the primary positive factor is the feeling and thought of the universal spirit of HU. This is the pure Spirit of Life, and, therefore, Its feeling and thought flow continually toward the increasing expression of livingness which is the specialization which we seek. It must be along a line affording it a center from which it may more perfectly realize this feeling and express this thought. In other words, the way to specialize the generic principle of ECK is by providing new mental conditions in consonance with its own orginal nature.

The individual can have his own personal reality, under these conditions, which is not subject to the laws of this physical universe. He is free to imagine anything such as living for years without eating, levitating, and he can by self-agreement, in cooperation with the ECK power, make mental pictures very real to himself. The scientific method of inquiry brings one to the conclusion that the required conditions for translating the racial or generic modus operandi into a specialized individual operation is a new way of thinking, adopting a new attitude and holding to this new attitude. It is a mode of thought occurring with, and not in opposition to, the essential forward movement of the creative Spirit Itself. This is what every savant, savior, and sage has tried to tell us.

This requires an entire reversal of the old concepts. But once you have the deep, inward conviction that God Is, that God is love, and that we are God's heir and coheir with ECK—that you and I are the divine—you are ready to turn to making your own reality. You have come into the knowledge that thought and feeling are causes, and forms and conditions are the effects.

Any person who cannot agree with the realities about him is out of communication with such realities, out of harmony with the Spirit within and without. Misunderstanding will develop and he will likely be on a downward trend. Anyone who insists that his is the only universe, the only reality, and who tries to make the physical universe and others' realities conform to his, will constantly create failure for himself, be unhappy and possibly develop into a neurotic individual. His fear that the influence of others will change his own world and will make him like those who conform so strongly to the physical world often drives him into being like what he fears.

Once we have grasped the principle mentioned, on which individual specialization of the generic law of the creative process is founded, it becomes a practical possibility and we drop off the fears and lower levels of nonsurvival. We come into the influence of the radiating HU, and can use the Sound itself for the manifestation of the ECK principle within each of us.

This method of attitude is not new. All saints sing of it. Beyond Kabir was Rama and the Vedas, and beyond that the mysteries of the early religions on earth. All students of the Divine Science have at one time or other studied them and each arrived at his own conclusions. The science has been handed down through the ages through various forms, the true meaning of which has been perceived only by a few. When anyone raises himself above the masses enough to perceive truth, he is then included in the universal order of the world of HU, but in a perfectly different way from what he had previously supposed; for, from his new standpoint he finds that he is included, not so much as a part of the general effect, but as part of general cause. When he perceives this, he sees that the method of his further advance must be by letting the general cause flow freely into his specific center. He seeks to provide thought conditions which will enable him to do so.

You come to realize that the power of Spirit manifests as intelligence in the adaptation of means to ends. That is how it is in the production of supply for the support of physical life, and in the maintenance of the race as a whole. True, though I, in my investigation, have met at every turn with individual failing, I have found in the end that there is no cosmic failure. I further learned that the apparent individual failure was itself a part of the cosmic process, and would diminish in proportion as I attained to the recognition of the Spirit principle of that process, and provided the necessary conditions to enable it to take a new starting point in my own individuality. This also applies to you and every other individual in this world.

A destroy-attitude is a mechanism in the service of the lower mind against the betterment of oneself. Whether this attitude is obsessively in force or used in some lesser mode, determines the degree of one's confusion. The condition to betterment of the self is to recognize Spirit as intelligence and trust It, and to remember that though It is expressed through us, It in no way changes Its essential nature, just as electricity loses none of its essential qualities in passing through the filament of a lightbulb.

In doing this I found or rather discovered this premise: That I, Soul, was a center of divine spiritual operation. And that divine power is always operating for fuller expansion and wider expression. This meant the production of something which was beyond what has always occurred before, something entirely new,

91

not included in the past but developed out of former experiences by orderly growth. Since the power cannot change Its inherent nature, It must operate in the same manner through each Soul; consequently, in anyone's universe of which he is himself the center, It moves forward to produce new conditions always.

This results in looking at the Divine in a new light, for not only is It creative, but also directive. It determines the actual forms which the conditions for Its manifestation will actualize, as well as supplying the energy for production. There is the relation between the individual and the real ECK power, the forming power. HU is the forming power under our direction throughout this universe whether we realize it or not, and we must learn to trust Its formative quality when operating from this new starting point in ourselves.

The question arises, this being so, what is my responsibility? Your responsibility is this—to provide a specific center around which the divine energies can play. You must take responsibility for each individual in the generic order of being. You should exercise upon the power a force of attraction in accordance to the innate pattern of your particular individuality. As you begin to realize the law of this relation, you, in turn, are attracted toward the ECK power along the lines of least resistance, that is, on those lines which are most natural to your special form of mind and position on the social and emotional scale.

We must accept responsibility, as Rebazar Tarzs and the ECK saints have told us, for our individual actions. For as we go along in life sending up certain aspirations there are results that have intensified our attraction to the ECK forces. They, then, begin to act both through us and around us in accordance with our aspirations. This is the natural action between the divine power and the individual Soul, and this shows us that our desires should not be directed to the acquisition of particular things so much as to the reproduction of spiritual activities within our universe in certain particular phases. This, being in its very nature creative, is bound to externalize into corresponding things and circumstances.

When these external facts appear in the outer world in our objective life, we must not cease to be interested, but accept the responsibility for their creation as our own and keep them going until they have run their course of usefulness as a part of our individual helpfulness to the whole. Too many fall short of completing their objective goals, and consequently accept only the responsibility for their externalized creations and failures. The creative method of visualization, or thinking with feelings, brings the materials and conditions for work into our hands. We must take the responsibility to use them with diligence and practicality.

One ought to become a knowing center of divine energy, and take the responsibility for doing so. If one does not, one may be on one hand trying to lead the center like a blind force, or on the other, be under a blind, unreasoning impulsion from the center. He will receive guidance because he seeks guidance and he both seeks and receives according to the operation of the principle which he is able to recognize; thus, he does not sacrifice his freedom or dwarf his power any more than an electrician does who uses electricity to apply it to some specific purpose. The more intimate one's knowledge of this reciprocal action becomes, the more he finds it leads him on to freedom. This is the same principle which we find in physical science; that nature obeys us precisely in the same degree to which we first obey nature. There is an ancient law, "What is truth on one plane is truth on all."

The key to this factor concerning Spirit, Soul, mind, body, and circumstances is in the new attitude which creates new conditions because it realizes the true order of the creative operation. If we want to bring life, beauty, and freedom into our lives, we must begin by bringing harmony and order into our thoughts. Then we find ourselves the starting point on a new creative line, not by force of personal will, but by the union with Divine Spirit, which in expression of its inherent love and beauty makes all things new.

Now we come to the points that prevent results. These are very simple. First, not really understanding who we are, the role that Spirit plays and further, not realizing that God or Spirit is love, justice, health, and is impersonally willing to answer those who truly make contact and cooperate with Spirit. Second, thinking that faith should make life easy and effortless, being resentful or antagonistic about difficulties instead of knowing they have been manifested in the life of those who set the forces into operation for a purpose and so must be accepted as such. Third, persistence in thinking that the divine power's desire for man is suffering, loneliness and misery, instead of knowing that Spirit is perfect and can only desire and give perfection; that imperfections result from not using the power of the Spirit. Still further by persisting in thinking that God has a special detail for each of us instead of knowing that when we make our own task we learn that positive results will be granted through the creative method of the all-giving Spirit. Finally, by living on the emotional scale of the lower levels where resentments, envy, jealousy and objection to any instruction, reproof and discipline hold sway instead of rising above all this by self-discipline finding that which one desires in the worlds of HU.

By filling our world with the creative sound of HU, the unknown name of God, we will become a channel for Divine Spirit. When used properly, uttered aloud or silently, the creative Soul will enable our Soul to ride the divine vibrations through all the realms of time and space to our own glorious destination.

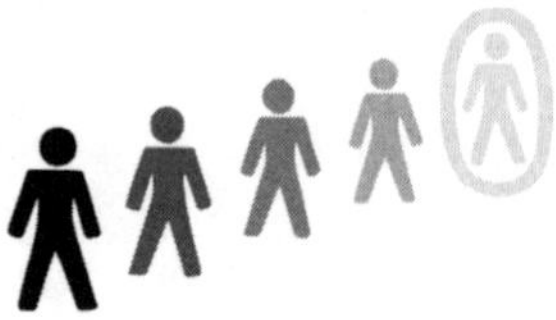

7

Book of the Laws

*T*here is always an implied set of unwritten laws the mystics, savants, and avatars speak about. This is entirely different from what Yaubl Sacabi or other ECK Masters taught their followers. As an example, we find John the Apostle saying Jesus could not give the truth, but only part of it, to the people, else they could not have contained it. Later he said again, "And there are also many other things which Jesus did, the which, if they should be written every one, I suppose that even the world itself could not contain the books that should be written." This is true of every spiritual giant who has come to this world.

Down through the ages man has not been able to contain truth, for it is hard for those who look for it with eyes that see the outer circumstances and have little inner belief. Certainly, belief must be a powerful postulate and conviction. You must feel strongly about what you know. If you have a strong feeling about it, then Spirit will openly operate through you. It is like the old saying "Strong feelings must be breathed into your convictions." Therefore, what you think with the whole of you, on the surface and deep down, eventually comes to pass and manifests. Soon you will begin to enjoy the thrill of truth and receive it in joyous abundance. There are three things necessary to the thrill of recognition or realization: (a) an awareness that God or Spirit is good, unchangeable, eternally good and that It is the sum total of all the good that has ever been, or is, or will be; (b) an awareness that you exist because It exists in you and that without It, you could not exist at all; (c) an ardent desire to unite with It so It can express Itself through you, to others. We must come to know Spirit as love before we can even be able to love others—for love is the way to realization.

This is a thought to remember. All people who are very reserved, closed up, wrapped in their own concerns and those of their immediate families, can never find truth as easily as those who are relaxed and have affinity for others. Such people can hardly use their visual powers for picturing a future at all. However, each of us has free will to choose what we think, and what we think within comes forth visibly in our lives without.

There are fundamental laws that govern this physical universe through Spirit. These were once taught by an ancient ECK sage named Mksha, who appeared on this earth some 35,000 years ago to teach the people of the Indus Valley. His first teaching was, "Life is only Spirit, and being spirit it has nothing." The understanding of this points out clearly that it has only intelligence with the peculiar ability to perceive, penetrate, survive, have causation, specialization, creativeness, beauty, love, and ethics.

Spirit is the all-penetrating power which is the forming power of the universes of HU. It is the immortal, unchanging source of life which only changes form regardless of what the world may be. It is the causative force which man has studied, written about, and can only know the exacting properties of, never actually acquiring total knowledge. We know that its modus operandi works peculiarly in exacting ways as do the mathematical formulas. Scientists and students of the holy works, all know this.

This Spirit, the Voice of HU—HU is often known as the Sugmad—which is the true name of God in the upper realms, has one great quality and that is to create effect. As It flows down through the worlds, from Its fountainhead in the center of all creation, far above this earth world, It needs distributors, and It works through Souls. Its life consists in this universe of thought and feeling. By this inner movement upon Itself, It throws out vehicles through which to function and these become living forms because of the inner principle which is sustaining them. Therefore, Spirit, with which we are concerned, is the life of thought and feeling in ourselves, the Soul, as the force, the distributing medium of Itself.

Once we have grasped the idea of Spirit as the great forming power, we seek It in Itself through receptiveness. This is not complex, as can be illustrated. Of course, there are many parts of the main wave of Spirit within this work—mainly positive, negative, and neutral—which have been given various names by the religions of the world, but you need not be confused by them. However, the greatest principle of Spirit is that It is flexible within Its own forming power and will work with man's cooperation as a reflecting unit. Provided that man works in accordance with Its proper qualities.

We come to the second law which is: Soul is the manifested individual beingness of this ECK Spirit. The individual Soul has been created out of this Spirit, with the ability to have free will, to make Its own choice, to be able to have opinions, intelligence, imagination, and to postulate and create. It must survive for It has immortality, being a part of the Spirit, and It must be a distributing agent for Spirit. These two factors It cannot escape, but as a distributing agent It can, from Its own free will, choose Its course with Spirit or not, which means that the aspect of Spirit which is chosen is selected knowingly or unknowingly, for the purpose of acting as a distributor.

The proper duty of the Soul, as we know, is to choose to distribute the positive, the survival qualities of Spirit for the betterment of Itself and others; to become whole again with the Spirit.

Life-forms, society's laws, and civilizations on every planet, world or plane are just what the Souls dwelling there have made them. Souls, themselves, as the creative agents of Spirit, have created forms and life everywhere, including space, time, energy, and matter. This is the reason that man has worshiped gods in ignorance. The spiritual hierarchy is hardly more than a group of Souls working on various levels to keep the world running and creating laws pertaining to the upkeep of their individual planet, or planet worlds and planes, by being the distributing agents of Spirit. They happen to know more than Souls who live in the social community and do it knowingly for the betterment of all.

This brings us to the third law of this universe: that which reverts back to Spirit—the Law of Polarity, the Law of Opposites. Without mountains there can be no valleys. Without shadows there can be no perception of light. There is no evil unless there is good. Without wisdom there is no ignorance, and without age there is no youth.

As long as Soul is fixed to a body, has accepted a body with or without responsibility, it is subjected to this law unless it becomes a knowing individual, unless it can be objective and see that it will be effect as long as it is under the negation of this law.

This is a two-edged law, the positive, active side, and the negative, reactive side. It contains a third part, of course, the passive, or the middle path.

Polarity simply means the state of opposition between any two related factors: light and darkness, heat and cold, material and immaterial, harmony and discord, positive and negative, north and south, male and female, etc.

The Chinese called this law the yang and yin; the yang being the positive, or male principle, and the yin being the negative, or female principle. Strangely, living in this world of force, we are constantly being trained in the art of becoming slaves of phenomena. Since being the negative means decay and death we are schooled less in the art of living than in the art of dying.

We, as the individual Soul, going in and out of bodies, have collected a subconscious mind which is filled with the junk, the negativeness carried along in our incarnations. It is the baggage that one carries with him unless relieved of it, or until he can take control over it. Its only purpose is reaction; it needs to be dominated. Anyone who lives on this side of the Law of Polarity is not free, but is one who is always reacting to circumstances, who is enslaved to reactive habits, who is always being exploited, and is desirous of materialistic factors.

Buddha said, "Desire is the source of all pain." He was speaking of the needs of the reactive self, for effect always creates desire. It is said that Gandhi's

101

passive resistance may have been the negative path, but it succeeded because it was positive. It is the principle of demonstrating that you can do without anything and it will be thrust upon you. Especially if you demonstrate that you will be abased or besmirched by something, you will for certain, be overwhelmed by it, because you will be a challenge to the whole materialistic world.

When one gains perfect knowledge of Spirit, he does not have to give up the physical body and subtle bodies at once. He has his choice of going on living here as long as he is in perfect harmony with Spirit as Its agent and is not bothered with the Law of the Opposites.

This law states that every phenomenon, on whatever scale and in whatever world it may take place, from molecular to cosmic phenomena, is the result of combining the meeting of the two, plus the third, which is the passive middle. This is not the passive element that you find in negation, but a balancing of the two. It is the path which Buddha called the "Middle Path" of which he preached so much during his life upon this planet. Scientific thought today realizes the existence of positive and negative forces and the necessity of the two for the production of phenomena; force and resistance, positive and negative magnetism, positive and negative electricity, male and female cells. But science has never raised the question of a third force. According to exact divine science, one force, or two forces, can never produce phenomena. The presence of the third is always necessary to produce any phenomenon. This neutral force is not easily accessible to direct observation and understanding.

The idea of the unity of the three in Absolute ECK forms the basis of the three worlds and of the ancient teachings. For example out of this came the tri-gods of India: Brahma, Vishnu, and Shiva, or the physical, astral, and mental as known in the Western world. Jesus called it the Father, Son, and Holy Ghost, and it became the trinity of Christianity. It is the blending of the three into one that makes the whole man within this universe.

Those who have understood these three forces have left a strange history of supernatural phenomena which has puzzled mankind. The early Christian saints were aware of this. One easily calls to mind the levitation of St. Francis, St. Teresa, and other Christian saints, the stigmatization of Therese Neumann, the appearance of Rebazar Tarzs in other parts of the world when his real physical body is in Kashmir, the intact body of St. Rose of Viterbo, which has remained thus for many centuries after death. There is the longevity of Yaubl Sacabi, the ECK Master, the timeless youth of Babaji, the Indian saint, the marvelous feats of Apollonius of Tyana who physically removed himself from death and appeared miles away. There are the trance sleepers of India, the ability of Hamid Bey to stay buried alive for days, Domenica Lazzari, the Italian woman, who never ate; and the Tibetan saint, Milarepa, who could fly through the air. These and thousands of other phenomena could be described.

The fourth law of this universe is the Law of Vibration, or Harmonics: This is the law that governs all the influences upon the Soul and body in this world, such as wavelengths, outflows from the planets, stars, and heavenly bodies; music; sound; color; and general harmonics. Under this principle falls karma, cause and effect and inflow and outflow.

Much as material science tries to deny the fact, it is true that astrology plays a tremendous role in the life of all living things on this planet. Each sign of the zodiac brings forth the truth of the influence of the twelve signs upon the physical body and character traits of man. The old Chaldeans left records of proof that all persons in their nation lived by a horoscope.

A happy thought lies here in what Krishna told Arjuna, in the Bhagavad Gita. "He who regardeth the dweller in the body as a slayer, and he who thinketh he is slain, both of them are ignorant. He slayeth not, nor is he slain. He is not born, nor doth he die; nor having been, ceaseth he anymore to be; unborn, perpetual, eternal and ancient, he is not slain when the body is slaughtered. Who knoweth himself indestructible, perpetual, unborn, undiminished, how can that man slay, O Partha, or cause to be slain?

"As a man, casting off worn-out garments, taketh new ones, so the dweller in the body, casting off worn-out bodies, entereth into others that are new. Weapons cleave him not, nor fire burneth him, nor waters wet him, nor wind drieth him away. Uncleavable he, perpetual, all-pervasive, stable, immovable, ancient, unmanifest, unthinkable, immutable, he is called; therefore, knowing him as such, thou shouldest not grieve."

We further this study by taking up harmonics which mainly have to do with sound. The ancients developed sound before any of the other studies of the Spirit. Thus, music became the first of the arts to be brought into existence. Music is only a branch of the song of the Sugmad, the HU, the all-existing. The ancients were aware of the retardation or the deflection of vibration according to their research of spirit. They incorporated this knowledge into a particular formula which has been preserved into modern times. In time this formula was applied to music and today we have it in the regular octave scale. Close observance shows the manifestation of the Law of Harmonics in vibrations of every kind including light, heat, chemistry, and other vibratory sciences.

The seven-tone scale is the formula of the universe which is connected with the optimum side of the tone scale, the colors, planets, metals, numbers, qualities, vowels, and symbols. However, each has its opposite. Also, it is connected with the seven spiritual streams that separate from the main current.

For example, let us work from the seven scales of music. Each octave, do-re-mi-fa-sol-la-ti, contains a good foundation for understanding the cosmic laws of vibrations. Each octave has an ascending octave, in which frequency of vibrations increase. Starting, we say, at a thousand vibrations a second, it would increase to two thousand in the second-second, on the same octave. Increasing its vibrations it moves out into the ether, to the parts of the world, into other planes. But as one goes along the scale, it is found to descend, after ti, and continue going around the scale again and again, until it makes a circle or something similar to a circle. This is true of the physical universe for nothing keeps a straight line and that is why we see nature's things, a tree or bush, growing in waving motions instead of straight lines.

Apply this to work, and we find that physical energy does the same, even mental energy has the same pattern. We soon learn that shortly after a period of energetic activity, strong emotion or right understanding a reaction comes; work becomes tedious, tiring, and moments of fatigue and indifference enter into the feelings. Then instead of right thinking we begin to search for a compromise, a suppression, or possibly an evasion of difficult problems; we reach the lower scale of the harmonic. Finally we become lost. This can be applied to civilization, science, literature, art, religions and all life phases. Now this means that there is a deviation of forces and that nothing in the physical world stays in the same place, or remains what it was; everything moves, everything is going somewhere, is changing inevitably, either develops or goes down, weakens, or degenerates. It can be said it moves either along an ascending or descending line of octaves. Ascent or descent is the inevitable cosmic condition of any action.

We deceive ourselves by looking at the outer appearance because we think of things remaining on the same level for a long time, and secondly we are apt to go down in tone when the vibrations are descending. The whole danger to the individual lies in the fact of not knowing—of being completely ignorant.

Ignorance is, of course, unawareness of something within one's universe and this leads to violation of the cosmic law, and often to superstition, to the worship of false gods. Of course, there are other factors, some of them being: the vibrations of the octaves set up can be obscured by stronger vibrations which intersect them or which go in opposite directions. Or the vibrations could be completely neutralized by stronger vibrations.

You see that the Law of Harmonics also enters into other things, as has already been said. For example, here is the way it works as given in outline form:

Music	Colors	Symbol	Planet	Metal	Numbers	Quality	Vowels
Do	Red		Earth	Iron	3	Strength Wrath Mastery	o
Re	Orange		Sun	Gold	1 4	Pride Faith Prana	i

Music	Colors	Symbol	Planet	Metal	Numbers	Quality	Vowels
Mi	Yellow	Soul	Mercury	Mercury	5	Intelligence	e
Fa	Green		Saturn	Lead	8	Temperance Gluttony	oo
Sol	Blue	Spirit	Jupiter	Tin Aluminum		Justice Envy	u
La	Indigo		Venus	Copper		Spirit Mind	ee
Ti	Violet		Moon	Silver		Inner Force Healing	e

On the emotional scale it goes from lower upward: Positive attitude, stability, free will, exhilaration, position for optimum action, union with Spirit and serenity of being.

We may try to envisage the spiritual current but we will be unable to do so unless we finally track it to its fountainhead. We may then fully grasp the fact of the truth of vibrations and that "God is Spirit."

Briefly, karma is a matter of vibrations and can be changed by changing the vibrations. This will be taken up in the next phase of law.

The fifth law of the physical universe is the Law of Attitudes, or the states of being. Frankly, everything that operates with the laws of this part is capable of performing miracles. Not will, but the power of imagination rules our actions in this universe. Coué was said to have discovered the important fact that every time will opposed the imaginative power, the latter won in an easy manner; the adepts taught this centuries before Coué was born.

Lai Tsi says, "I have learned to stand back and let the Divine work through me." We find that this is the simple way of doing it—reaching the divine power for working through ourselves.

The power is within us and working, but most teachers want to show the way through some stupendous means. Yet the fact is that the power is easily contacted by anyone who will believe this. So easily, that the intellectual types often have a job accepting this while the more childlike ones leap on ahead of them.

Frankly, it is not necessary to have a Master to make contact with this power. Many people who have gained insight into truth did not have a teacher. Rebazar Tarzs told us that the spirit of truth would always be with us, and then, "He will lead you into all truth."

In my diaries are many notes on making contact with Spirit without the help of a Master. However, I have studied under many; at times I was confused, at other times things were made exceedingly clear. But one thing impressed me greater than all other things. That was: I found when adopting a certain attitude that I made contact with this power. It was an attitude of curious, childlike devotion to the great Spirit and if held for an unusual length of time, contact would manifest. I would become the operator of the Spirit power.

This is exceedingly important—this childlike attitude, for we find that the spiritually great hold this attitude, certain of what it will do, not for themselves, but for others. Read the history of any spiritual giant and you will find that he is or was of this nature: like St. Francis, Pythagoras, Socrates, Rama, Akhenaton, Confucius, and others who are outstanding examples of the childlike state of mind.

Now briefly, so many people want this childlike state but the urgency of their physical needs causes tension and fear thus closing the channel between themselves and the Spirit. Anxiety and fear are tense emotions, fastening the person rigidly into the emotional plane of consciousness so that he cannot reach the spiritual plane where things come true.

Competition intensifies the attitude of tension; tension springs from fear; fear rises out of excessive self-love; excessive self-love cuts one off from the contact with the ECK; thus, the qualities leading to satisfaction, happiness and growth are not achieved.

Once you realize the importance of you, Soul, and your value to ECK, as a distributor of the Divine, you will relax. You will no longer want to grasp things before others can have them, nor to influence the will of others so that they favor you. Instead, you turn to this Spirit and merge with it, merge with all the forces as well as the ECK in others. Anyone who recognizes his own self, as Soul, relaxes at once, for he can truly say, "I and the Father are one."

In this relaxed way, all channels from within are opened. Without causing injustice to anyone, the Spirit of you reaches out in Spirit, touching the Spirit of those who are concerned in the fulfilling of your needs, and increases your ability for helping others.

It is not as hard as one thinks!

Briefly, the Law of Attitudes goes like this. It is the corrected feeling and pictures you carry in your mind constantly. If you decide to take a picture with a camera—let's say of a tree, and do so, you view the pictured tree in the viewfinder. After a few days you get the pictures back from the camera shop, and you are not surprised to find that it's really a picture of a tree you took.

This is, simply, the same way life works. When we think, when we image something in our minds, we are sighting pictures in the viewfinder of the mind. The thought vibrations within us will deal with the exposed films we have made and presently the finished picture comes into visibility in our lives. It's as simple as that.

Now for the next law: the Law of Facsimiles which is an overlaying of the Law of Attitudes. This is the sixth law of the physical universe.

Now facsimiles deal with those pictures you took in the mind. These pictures have been with you since you came into the world. They are filed away by Soul, like cards in a little niche in the Soul's body, sometimes called the picture bank if filed in the Mental body. Generally, facsimiles are either borrowed or they are one's own. One can have either or both through a compulsive basis or on an unknowing basis. They will influence him in one way or another. If borrowed facsimiles become strong enough, they will influence him as though they were ones he had made of his own experiences, instead of facsimiles which he had made of the facsimiles of other beings' experiences. This is the real danger of too much reading; one is apt to start considering the experiences of the author as his own.

These facsimiles are merely little units of energy which gather about the body, mind, and Soul. They keep the attention of the individual "I" on them, especially if they are bothersome pictures. This is what oriental religion keeps calling karma.

The facsimile can control the individual to an extent that he becomes aberrated, and often in the old religions, especially among the savages, it was believed that an evil spirit had taken hold of him. The witch doctor would hold a ritual for the victim and take his attention from the pictures and by conviction he would become able again.

Of course the flows of energy which are recorded in facsimiles are dead flows. In order for them to have any power or life, a new flow of attention must be played over them by the individual. So you see that no matter what is wrong with the individual, he is the one who is keeping it that way. This comes in with cause and effect. When one is on a low level, he fails in his beingness. He is existing on death wishes, with qualities of unbeingness. The chief aspects of cause and effect are the positive and negative. When an individual is cause he is being positive; when he is effect he is being negative. The art of good picturization is the art of full beingness.

The seventh law of the physical universe is: the Law of Unity, thinking in the whole instead of in parts. It is a simple way of knowing the solution to the problem the instant it presents itself. In a way this is called liberation from the bondage of the world, which men have always cried to their God to give them.

This law simply means that one must be wholly within the ECK in order to enjoy himself as the whole man and be able to select consciously what he wants in life and work at it.

It is having a certainty, an intuitiveness on what one desires to know at a particular moment. Then ECK is leading the way, giving the individual a beneficial life under that person's choice in full freedom.

Many people know how to meet life in a relaxed manner, changing their attitudes to solve problems. Others are tense, put a mental grip on their attitude and will not let go. They want to change their lives yet they dare not change their attitude. This happens because they have built up a particular way of thinking, because it seemed, in the abstract, to benefit them. However, it in practice prevents them from achieving their goals and though they become increasingly aware of this, they still hold on tensely and there is no improvement in their circumstances. They don't want to lose the benefit which for years they have

111

thought their way of thinking brought them. Only by losing the illusionary benefits of their mistaken thought can they win the transcendent life they believe is possible.

Mainly, the way into wholeness is by certainty. Jesus outlined this in his words, "For verily I say unto you, That whosoever shall say unto this mountain, Be thou removed, and be thou cast into the sea; and shall not doubt in his heart, but shall believe that those things which he saith shall come to pass; he shall have whatsoever he saith."

It is possible for one to be a channel of the Divine Spirit through belief and strong feelings. By this method alone can wonders be worked, for words and actions will be of great power, and when one feels strongly about this—there can be nothing in this world which can shake him of this faith. Then belief becomes a powerful conviction. Every spiritual giant, saint, and adept has had this faith of conviction. Only believe!

This creates a vibration of its own, an atmosphere around you, which will continue to grow until others start noticing it, and your growth will be in leaps and bounds.

You should have a good picture of the Real Self, the individual that is really you—Soul. Yes, it is also vital to have a good clear picture, an absolute conviction— of the resources of the Divine Spirit. This Spirit is endless, as I have told you constantly. All things pour forth from this great intelligence, this source of all. Once you realize this, once you have a vivid mental picture of this limitless power and might—once you visualize It—you naturally have complete confidence in It and then wonders begin to happen.

The secret of the Law of Unity lies in the fact that any problem the individual has, is always a personal problem. Since divine power is infallible, that is, incapable of making a mistake, it is the individual use of this power which creates the mistakes.

You can realize yourself how many mistakes can be made when the attention is scattered. Divine power concentrates on the least of things, so how much more upon its great creation—man. Be assured of this. This means that you must not let outer circumstances get so much of your attention and activity that you cannot pause, take time and lean upon the ECK power. Thus is your world created.

Many people think that in visualization one sees with the inward eyes just as they do with their outer eyes. This is not so. It is more of a kind of feeling. Visualization is a great thrill of expectancy like the young wife who hurries to the airport to meet her husband after he has been away for months. She lives it as she drives along the highway, seeing his face in her imagination, feeling his kiss and his embrace. There is ecstasy in the feeling—you can have the same for yourself in feeling that the power is giving you wholeness.

This is the magic that Jesus taught us. Yes, a magic of being absolutely certain about yourself in God. Willpower has nothing to do with this. All that is required is that you admit that you are human, alone, have no power, but that you believe your thoughts can form a mold in which the ECK power, indwelling you in your kingdom within, fills your life and being. Then you state a truth that the whole of you can believe on your surface mind and deep inside.

It is practical then that you do not make efforts with the will to reach this belief. You are a part of the divine power so your thought forms a mold which the power instantly fills with life. Therefore, what you think with the whole of you, on the surface and deep down, inevitably comes to pass and manifests.

You see, it is all perfectly logical and there is no need to have any qualms in believing any thing so clear and obvious.

This is the Law of Unity. This is the book of laws!

8

The Appeal of Man to God

*M*an has always appealed to God in his dire necessity, but forgets It when his stomach is full and outer circumstances are pleasing. A man without particular needs does not feel the necessity of prayer.

The law of ECK says that everything must be paid for, and it must be paid in proportion to what is received; though man usually thinks to the contrary. He will pay quickly for trifles or things that are perfectly useless; for something valuable, he haggles; a clear understanding of this must come of itself, and until it does, man will come to God appealing for help.

The orthodox philosophies are no help to man in this understanding. He must on his own take the step in search for the ECK. He must come to know that through thinking or feeling he can make a mold: unthinkingly he is constantly making the wrong kinds of molds every day. You see how essential it is to make the right molds deliberately, and how important right thinking is.

Man must come to know that the ECK is the source of all; the creator of all things. Once he has grasp of this he is ready to learn to make himself a channel for the flow to fulfill his needs.

Maeterlinck said, "The man for whom the hour of misfortune has sounded is caught up by an invisible whirlwind, and for years back have these powers of the ECK been combing the innumerable incidents that must bring him to the necessary moment, to the exact spot where tears be in wait for him."

In a later statement he observed that "scarcely has the disaster befallen one that he has the strange sense, the sensation of having obeyed an eternal law."

Through observation we come to realize the fact that every experience we have encountered, every pleasure, pain, triumph, and disappointment, is the precise working out of the cause to which it was due. Voltaire remarked that chance is a word devoid of meaning, and Schiller wrote "There's no such thing as chance; and what to us seems merest accident springs from the deepest source of destiny."

This is not a problematical theory, or a matter of speculation, but a fundamental truth. The outer self is like the prodigal son who went out from the presence of his father and lived with the swine. The real "I" remained with the father to whom the father said: "Son, thou art ever with me, and all that I have is thine."

It is necessary to bring back the outer self, the prodigal son, to the happiness and perfection of the father's home, the Real Self. By living in the consciousness and knowledge of that Real Self, one gradually brings back the outward self, so that it rests upon the support of the Divine Spirit within.

Soon it will be seen that much of the knowledge that philosophers teach is purely mental knowledge effective primarily on the mental plane. Spiritual knowledge is properly concerned with Soul and Its unseen force. Such knowledge has to be realized and the meaning understood within the depth of one's own being. We are really little children learning the meaning of things that we already know and do not understand.

Truth is original. In time you will learn, as all who have gotten a glimpse of it have, that long training of the self will develop the ability of raising the vibration pattern to a plane where direct contact can be made with limitless intelligence.

Rebazar Tarzs spoke of the existence of this ability and the higher plane when he said, "I have much to say to you, but you cannot accept it all now. When the ECK enters into you, It shall lead you to truth." This points out that all can find that gift of Spirit within himself by effort, persistence, and self-discipline.

If you are having great joy in your spiritual life, but the physical and mental life is not receiving adequate attention, this is a stolen joy based on illusion rather than full realization. The fact is, that when we make complete contact with the Spirit, all our needs are met on all planes. This apparent joy in the spiritual life is based more on higher emotions than on spiritual consciousness. To merge spiritually with God is to receive on every plane; for, the windows of heaven are open to all, for all.

Those who make the mistake of thinking that higher emotions are merely the silent realms of spiritual consciousness attribute their failure to receive supply for their physical needs to the idea that it is God's will for them to be unsupplied on the physical plane. However, God is the unchanging spiritual power, almighty, ever present and eternal. Its will is unchanging, and Its will is that man have delight in It and have his heart's desire. Not as a reward to man, but simply because it is impossible to contact It without receiving an abundant flow of all good things from It. It is a glorious realization to know that nothing can separate you from God.

There is a wonderful story about a Hindu adept, Coomra Sami, who lived in the Valley of Kashmir. A great European medical doctor once visited him for instructions in Sami's way. He spent several months with the strange adept who had lived in the West and knew the Europeans quite well. He taught the doctor that life is a continual succession of opportunities to be taken advantage of or lost, that every physical process leaves permanent imprints on Soul through the nervous system, and every process leaves permanent imprints on the body.

His teachings stressed that every course of action can be traced to its source. Imagination is brought into action primarily by an abstract production of the mind which is called an ideal. At the back of every action lies a more or less clear ideal, which gives the key to every man's outlook on life as well as to his individuality. "In every man this ideal differs," said the adept.

The key to adeptship is fashioned from a single truth. Whoever is in love with his ideal will make the greatest effort of which he is capable in order to fulfill the demands of that urge. From this we see that the full power of the wills is called into action by a definite and overwhelming incitement. We can now grasp the meaning and purpose of existence, and persuade ourselves that the greatest good, the maximum bonum of the old philosophers, is within our reach—that the kingdom of heaven is within. It is possible to achieve our purposes by a steadfast holding to the ideal. We can now give up the individual will to the Divine Will and be carried into the kingdom.

118

After six months of these wonderful teachings, the doctor decided to leave. The adept said to him: "If you plan to go to Tibet to seek further, I tell you that you will not find it there, nor anywhere else. The path lies within you, in the depths of your consciousness. You will find it nowhere but within you. Seek there. Go no further!"

Briefly, these are the phases of thinking that the individual goes through for growth. When reading them, you will not want to recognize yourself and make the change. Hardly any of us do. We are afraid we will lose the benefit of our mental state, even if it is false and has produced circumstances we wish to change.

The phases of growth, from misdirected thinking to right thinking, falls into these main groups. They have numerous other descriptions, however, so an exact description of one's own may not be here. It will be close enough for you to recognize your own, in detail, from these broad outlines if you want to recognize it. By this time you ought to know that it is the only way to change circumstances you do not wish to be present in your life. Briefly, we'll list them, again:

1. Wrong thinking, causing as it does, physical, nervous, and mental handicaps, provides a way of escape from normal living. It allows a person to withdraw from normal activities and responsibilities. He thinks, deep in his heart, he is as capable as others. Deep down, he does not want to understand any teaching which would abolish his way of escape.

2. Wrong thinking which appears to offer benefits of some kind is not going to be given up. The person is likely to resist teachings which lead to the giving up of an error-producing thought process and to feel antagonistic to the teacher. He may try to win the

sympathy or indulgence of the teacher. He may seek to discredit the motives of the teacher. He may attempt to put the responsibility for making decisions in everyday life on the teacher instead of changing his thinking processes and dealing personally with the problem.

3. Wrong thinking is usually born along with feelings of inferiority. This becomes apparent when the person tries to maintain an attitude of intellectual superiority. He rationalizes away the facts of his failure to change his unwanted circumstances in life. He attempts to substitute intellectual argument for actual practice of the truth. He will use illness, or his failure, to fasten the sheltering, ministering attentions of someone else on himself and attempt to make that person feel guilty at the thought of abandoning him to his own devices.

4. Wrong thinking makes a person feel uncomfortable and out of place, when right thinking people are around. It will result in a person feeling depressed, feeling self-pity, feeling envious, resentful or antagonistic toward those who succeed in any degree in truth.

5. Wrong thinking leads a person to feel shut in and lonely. He begins to want to hear of other people who are also thinking in the wrong way; who are ill, depressed, unsuccessful, resentful, moody, or he will have a special interest in people who take refuge in superiority.

6. Wrong thinking, being a habit of years, is difficult to give up. Such a person will have an inward resistance to self-discipline and persistence, and will reveal this by insisting that he has faith but that it does not work for him, because he is different from others. Or he insists that he has followed all instruc-

tions to the letter, has had no results whatever, and has not the faintest idea why he alone should fail. Or he states that he cannot concentrate, hasn't time, cannot remember or grasp the teachings.

These are a broad outline of the phases through which some people pass on their way to union with God. Provided they pass through them all is well—the danger is staying in any one of them permanently.

One does not need to believe to listen to the words of those who know. Knowledge is power, and if one desires to grow in wisdom and power let him put himself into the state of mind—that he knows nothing and start from that point. Then shall he have wisdom more abundantly; yet not until then will he receive it. All the things we see are the ECK power in form and substance.

The application of using yourself as a channel for divine power must be a personal one, for it is only through the individual that the higher specialization of the power can take place. However, do not suppose that you, yourself, bring the creative force into being. To support this is an inversion, and we cannot impress upon ourselves too deeply that the relation of the individual to the ECK Spirit is that of a distributor, and not that of the original creator.

What, then, is the power which we are to distribute? It is the ECK power, the originating Spirit Itself. We are certain of the fact that everything has its origin in Spirit, and is Spirit.

We must assume, as an axiomatic fact, that what we are to distribute, or differentiate into manifestation is nothing else than Truth, or Spirit.

Hence, it is evident that the purpose of the distribution must be the more perfect expression of Spirit as that which It is Itself, and what It is, in Itself, is life. That which is seeking for expression, then, is the perfect livingness of Spirit, the creativity of beingness, or whatever you desire to call It.

We find that physical life is only one mode of Spirit's manifestation. Physical life is the completion of a great creative series of actions, assigning life in different forms in a great evolutionary movement.

By thinking, you act as a distributor of ECK power, and form a mold. For this reason you must see that it is essential to make deliberate right molds. Here is a key to failure or success in this physical world.

In the unseen, great changes take place once you make the mold and the ECK fills it with life. It remains in the womb of the unseen until the day of its birth comes, at which time it will be born and you and all others will see it. There is nothing fanciful or emotional about this. It is an exact science based on unchanging law. Using it we are able to manifest our desires, as well as anyone else.

There are stumbling blocks to this. First is the "conviction" that visualization is too difficult to be achieved. This is not true. So many writers give the impression that it is very difficult and that it is a dark secret. Visualization is easy. Anyone can do it.

Secondly, is the idea that things should immediately get easier for you when you thought-build. This is not true. If you have been indulging in wrong thinking for years and have built wrong thoughts and things, they often have to work themselves out before something better can come into your consciousness.

The reason that many people do not achieve success in prayers or affirmatives is that they believe that they, themselves, are the receptacles of the channel. If we really trust Spirit to supply us with whatever we need, no matter how difficult it may seem to acquire, we won't worry about holding on to what we have in order to get more. You cannot close the channel at the out-going end and keep it open at the in-going end. If you close one end, both close.

Acceptance level is the next phase to discuss. What can you accept from life? Does your life consist of having only that which is on the lower level of the economic scale? How can you be a positive cause in the free flow of the ECK force?

This leads us into conditions of existence which are circumstances, and qualities of life. They could be called apparency, reality, and livingness. One condition is being, which is the assumption or choosing of a category or identity. Another condition is doing; that is, action, function, accomplishment, attainment of goals, fulfilling of purpose and changing position in space. The other condition is having; that is, owning, possessing, being capable of commanding, positioning, taking charge of objects, energies, spaces. Having is, also, being able to touch, to permeate and direct the disposition of something. Beingness is probably the highest of the human virtues. It is more important to be able to permit or allow other people to have identity than to be able to assume an identity one's self.

Acceptance is the opposite of rejection. Acceptance enables one to possess at any level of reception, to act out the wish as though fulfilled already.

In the physical expression of life in this solar system, space seems to express the idea of being; energy, that of doing; and time, that of having. Time, then, is a barrier of acceptance. One determines a change in time as a change in what one has. This is a crude form of a very profound idea.

In our modern world we have developed so much emphasis on money, that it has become a barrier to understanding the law of flow. Our society has become committed to the process of multiplying its wants. We have abnormally developed and stimulated the accumulative instinct so that we have actually come to look upon life as little more than an opportunity of piling up matter, much as rubbish, in the shape of so-called material possessions.

The stuff of existence is constantly changing and time is a way to express this mattering of existence. One can be free or a slave in regard to time in his life's record. The best way to learn about what one has, that is, time, is to look. Our society has fallen into a pattern of not confronting or looking at what is wrong with the life which it has developed. Soul will put up with anything rather than have nothing. Pain is more desirable than nothing.

This age tells us that many things are not good to have and the individual gets into the habit of fighting nothing. He takes pills for what he doesn't actually have and to balance the scale he gets sick and loses material things as well as subjective things. Good and bad are considerations, opinions, and depend upon agreement.

Being the things you desire and acting it out is the principle. This comes directly into the area of consciousness. One just knows that it is coming about, feels it and acts it. A full easy knowing is acceptance of the desire: feeling it puts desire into action; acting manifests it. So you have here an eminently practical formula. Know, feel, and act.

Sudar Singh said to me once, "To enter into the realm of God, one must be spiritually bold and adventuresome!"

The timid never find true love and happiness, but the bold do. If you can feel and image forth the wildest things in your mind, perhaps riding a spaceship through the skies, you can have that experience, simply by knowing, feeling, and acting the part.

The more unreal anything seems, the more unreal it will become and conversely, the more real it is, the more real it becomes. It is said that this universe works in reverse. To get what you want, become external or exterior; to get what you don't want, collapse, become involved. The physical universe runs backward. If you begin to examine time and the physical universe, they suddenly become real and big; you are collapsing in it; reverse this and you will remain exterior to it and will see and accept time and the universe for what they are.

This is not a mysterious principle beyond man's understanding. It is pure logic, as all true principles are. Living within the consciousness we find that ECK then works through us as the distributing factor, is the worker of miracles and will work miracles in your life, too, if you find it within and preserve the harmony of perfect faith.

When we realize the truth of the creativeness of ECK, then we see that the originating ECK is not physical, but Its expression consists in thought and feeling and acting out the part.

If we have grasped the idea of the ECK power as the great forming force, we shall seek it in the fountainhead of form as well as of power. As a logical deduction, we shall look to It to give form to our thoughts and feelings. If the principle is once recognized, the sequence is obvious. The form taken by our outer conditions, whether of body or circumstance, depends on the form taken by our thoughts and feelings, and our thoughts and feelings will take form from that source which is allowed to them according to our acceptance level.

Accordingly, if we allow our thoughts and feelings to accept their fundamental suggestions from the relative and limited, they will assume a corresponding form and transmit this to our outer environment, thus repeating the old order of limitation in a ceaselessly recurring round. This brings about the objective of getting out of this circle of limitation, and the way to do it is to remold our thoughts and feelings into new forms, continually advancing to greater perfection. This is what the ECK Masters call "perfection of Soul."

To meet this requirement there must be a forming power greater than our own unaided conception, and this is to be found in our realization of the ECK as the supreme beauty or wisdom, molding our thoughts and feelings into shapes harmoniously adjusted to the fullest expression, in and through us, of the expression which ECK is in Itself.

The principle which we look for is indeed simple—that of receptiveness. What is needed is the placing of one's self in a receptive mental attitude toward the divine ECK with the intention of receiving Its forming influence into our mental or Soul substance. An example of this is—it is always the presence of a definite intention that distinguishes the intelligent, receptive attitude of mind from a merely spongelike absorbency, which sucks in any and every influence that may happen to be floating around. We must not shut our eyes to the fact there are various influences in the mental surroundings, and some of them are most undesirable.

Clear and definite intention is as necessary in our receptive attitude as in our active and creative one; if our intention is to have our own thoughts and feelings molded into such forms as to express those of the Spirit, then we must establish that relation to the

ECK which by the conditions of the case, must necessarily lead us to the conception of new ideas vitalized by a Divine Power which enables us to bring them into concrete manifestation.

It is in this way that we become differentiating centers of the divine power giving It expression in form in the world of space, time, energy, and matter. Thus is solved the great problem of enabling the ECK to act upon the plane of the particular, without being hampered by the limitations which the mere physical law of manifestation imposes on it. It is here that consciousness performs the function of a bridge between the finite and infinite as noted before. It is for this reason that a recognition of its susceptibility to impression is so important.

You understand then, that by establishing a personal relation to the life of ECK, the sphere of the individual becomes enlarged.

It was Vipula, an ECK sage, who said, "An external thing will have its effect according to the nature and purity of the consciousness."

Upon this knowledge, the individual boldly allows a greater intelligence than his own to take the initiative, and since he knows that this intelligence is also the very principle of Spirit Itself, he cannot have any fear that It will act in any way to the diminution of his individual life, for that would be to stultify Its own operation. It would be self-destructive action which is a contradiction to the conception of creative Spirit.

We must approach every individual as the "I" with an almost religious awe of his potentialities. There should be an absence of grades, or levels, which create a problem for our society prone to dissect and condition life to its own conformed ideas. The only thing that rates is Divine Spirit, intelligence, and we have no way of measuring or appraising It. It works, and we must accept It as It is. Thus, we find that consciousness, once it has accepted this, will create the will to participate in Divine Spirit more and more, not just on occasions.

Knowing then, that by Its inherent nature, Spirit will work to the expansion of the individual's consciousness, one can rest upon It with the utmost confidence and trust It to take an initiative that will lead to far greater results than any we can forecast from the standpoint of our knowledge. As long as we insist on dictating the particular form which the action of the ECK is to take, we limit It, and so close ourselves to avenues of expression which might otherwise be open to us. Should we question ourselves as to the reason we do this, we shall find that in the last resort it is because we do not believe in ECK as a constructive and forming force.

We have advanced to the conception of It as an executive force, which will work to a prescribed pattern, but we have yet to grasp the conception of It as versed in the art of design and capable of elaborating schemes of construction, which will not only be complete in themselves, but in perfect harmony with one another.

When we advance to the conception of the ECK as contained in Itself the ideal of form as well as power, we shall cease from the effort of trying to force things into particular shape, whether on the inner or outer plane, and shall be content to trust the inherent harmony, the beauty of ECK to produce combinations far in advance of anything we could have conceived in ourselves.

This, of course, is not reducing one's self on the emotional scale to the state of apathy in which all desires, expectations and enthusiasms have been halted, for these are only the mainsprings of our physical machinery, but on the contrary, one's action will be quickened by the knowledge that there is working at the back of him a formative power so infallible that It cannot miss Its mark. This leaves one in the attitude that regardless of how beautiful life may be now, there is always something better to come. It will come by the natural law of Spirit, for Spirit, in Itself, is the principle of increase.

We must realize that conditions will grow out of present conditions for the simple reason that if we are to reach some further point, it can only be started from where we are now in the present moment.

Thus, the only factor that is attached to this thought is that we are required to cooperate with ECK, and this cooperation consists of making the best of existing conditions in cheerful reliance on the use of ECK in Its ability to increase and express Itself through us, because we are in harmony with It. We revert back to the original point, the state of attitude in which consciousness dwells. For example, the old sage who wrote the Psalms said in the 91st Psalm, "He that dwelleth in the secret place of the most High shall abide under the shadow of the Almighty!" Then he goes on to explain the protection and the goodness of life that the ECK gives when we dwell in the consciousness, the secret place of the most High.

This mental attitude is of immense value in setting the individual free from worry and anxiety; as a consequence, our lives become more efficient and happier. We must work for work's sake, trusting to ECK, and we shall find the secret of cooperation is to have faith, a certainty in ourselves because we have complete confidence in ECK. Soon we find that this divine self-confidence is something different from an egotistical boasting of the outer self which tries to assume personal authority over Spirit.

Recognize the Life of Spirit as well as the Law of Spirit. The two are identical and cannot be separated and cannot deny themselves.

The path of Soul is therefore plain. It is simply to contemplate the life, love, and beauty of divine power and affirm ourselves as already giving expression to It as a channel, in thought, feeling, and action, however insignificant they may appear in the present. This path is very narrow and humble in its beginning, but it ever grows wider and mounts higher, for it is the continually expanding expression of the action of Spirit which is infinite and knows no limit.

Therefore, man's appeal to God is: "How can I become a channel for thy great work?"

The answer is simple. Think, feel, and act. That is all there is to it, when combined with beauty, love, and wisdom.

9

The Shape of the Altar

*A*lthough I have found many saints are meta-
physically reticent, most of them are not.
However, it's mostly a problem of communication. They have discovered, they claim, a unique something for which there is no word or name. It does not
belong to the world in which language is born, for the
universe is its by-product and nothing exists without it.

Whatever they have discovered is their own particular individual understanding of the Divine Spirit
and Its modus operandi. Their usual pattern of telling
about it is to use a sign or a name of their own designation, yet having the same meaning after all—that
of the divine power, or Spirit. Because of this, many
holy men seem to differ in their opinions of the power;
however, it is only a matter of terminology. The theory
being that if one starts toward communication with
Spirit, he should follow that path to the end. I personally disagree with this for each individual is different
from the other. Each individual must find his own
path, his own belief. If not, he will likely spend excessive effort and time practicing a system which is not
suited to him.

The individual will go constantly to the altar for communication with Spirit, only to one day suddenly learn that he has been practicing a method which is not of his nature under any circumstance.

Throughout the Old Testament the altar is prominently mentioned as the place where the people worshiped. The altar is a symbol of the consciousness, the individual "I" where the thoughts and feelings of man retire to worship the Divine Spirit, the inner part of Him and his Being.

In this physical universe dealing with outside circumstances the average chela does not find Occam's razor, a great principle discovered by William of Occam, serviceable; but that is his mistake. He even neglects the Spiritual Exercises of ECK. Even those who are concerned with expropriating vast cosmic ideas, often in a burst of Faustian energy, worsen their condition by trying to solve sweeping universal problems that better trained and more competent investigators would deliberately avoid over a period of time.

So, then it comes to this point—are you willing to undertake the mammoth task of seeking God as did Buddha and Mahavira (Nataputra, founder of Jainism), or spend endless hours in meditation and trance as did Sankara and Sri Aurobindo Ghose, the Hindu mystic? If not, then you might try another method of learning the modus operandi, as Fubbi Quantz taught directly to his inner circle.

We know the way is difficult for those who pick and choose. The best method is to avoid like or dislike. Rebazar Tarzs speaks of going into the inner chamber for Soul Travel. This means worshiping at the inner altar, where consciousness of the individual kneels before the ECK in true humbleness and says, "I surrender my will to you, O Lord. Do what you will with me."

The cosmic altar of God is real; it is shaped as needed in each individual case. To get into mystical union with the divine ECK is illuminating and basic. When one puts himself in position to worship at the altar he finds an understanding of life, omnipotence of the Eternal and God's friendliness to man. He learns the difference between head knowledge and heart wisdom. All truth is in this world now. It is within the altar, hidden deeply within, and when we come to know the shape of the altar, we see that God is love. We have all lived for eternity; for eternity has no beginning and no end. It is, in fact, an endless circle of beingness; so, live for eternity, too. During this time we have not always realized that we are the temples of God wherein dwells the ECK. We have shaped God's power by our conscious thoughts and created for ourselves all manner of chaos.

When a man thinks of himself as separate from the ECK, an obvious impossibility, since he lives in God and in It has his being, he moves and falls out of the secret place of safety and harmony. His wrong thoughts, words, and actions build a record of themselves into the atmosphere surrounding him. This atmosphere is magnetic, so it attracts like to itself. Therefore, if a man has created an atmosphere of chaos, he will be attracted to a spot where chaos will come, e.g., accidents and disasters. This is what is meant by "Be not deceived; God is not mocked: for whatsoever a man soweth, that shall he also reap." This is the law of our universe. Cause and effect is what it is.

Most people are unawakened and have not realized the chaos created by their thoughts of separateness from ECK. Thousands and millions of devout people are not aware of who they are, and the words of the ECK Masters: "Whatever works we do, you shall do also" would seem blasphemy to them, if anyone but the Master had spoken.

Once, Rebazar Tarzs said to me during a visit in his spiritual body, "To understand the Spirit is to understand life eternal; for to live in the physical body is to be imprisoned, but to be able at will to leave the body and travel into the worlds hitherto unknown is a pure joy." All this knowledge of the Spirit is much more easily acquired than most people imagine. They do not realize that it is first necessary to have faith. Are we not told that "to him that believeth all things are possible?"

To take this a stage further, the common belief that a mystic, yoga, saint, or adept can transport his own physical body one place to another through space is considered impossible by those sunk in materiality. Yet it is true. For example, this feat was performed by Apollonius of Tyana, who was given his death warrant by Domitian, the tyrant, while standing before the throne in Syracuse. Then he, Apollonius, suddenly disappeared in full sight of the assembly of the court, to be seen again shortly afterward at Puteoli near Mount Vesuvius.

As for my own experiences, I am often visited at night by Rebazar Tarzs in my own apartment, although I know he is some six thousand miles away in the Hindu Kush Mountains. I have felt his grip on my hands, seen the cushions in the chair sink under his weight and smelled the fragrance of his flesh. Paramahansa Yogananda tells of a visit from his master Sri Yukteswar, who had passed on years before. He experienced touching his master's body and found its flesh firm and hard as though in real physical life. These are not impossible phenomena, but ordinarily we think so. Throughout the history of the Christian church we find records of similar events, and the power of the Catholic saints.

Peering into the secret of the divine power, the insight of God, Itself, we find that from which all vibrations emanate. In order to reach this place, the secret altar of the Self, we, who desire wisdom, must put ourselves into a stage of knowing nothing, a child-like state. By doing so we attain wisdom most abundant, but not until then will we receive it. To him that hath, more shall be given, but from him that hath not, shall be taken away even that which he seems to have.

This brings us to the study of vibrations.

In the beginning I want to reiterate that ECK is everywhere, as all the students of Eckankar know. It operates on wavelengths. Do you realize the significance of the word, vibration? When we talk of the movement of a tree branch in the wind, we are hinting at a fundamental, at a great truth which underlies all life. Pythagoras was really the first man to tell us that the Earth was round and not flat. And he gave us a greater truth; that everything in this world, both the visible and invisible, vibrates.

Every wavelength can be felt, detected by ordinary physical and sensory means, such as the vibrations of a car or of a person. For instance, when one gently touches the finger of another a distinct vibration can be felt passing from one hand to the other. In this way a man who is both blind and mute, even deaf, can know one individual from another. A dog will know its master from a stranger in the dark; it will know who is its enemy and who is friendly. No two parts of a life-form, of an individual or of an animal have the same vibration, the same wavelength; never does one plant have the same wavelength as another.

The whole life of the individual is one great wave-length, vibration. The body ceases to have a certain wavelength when it dies, but Soul, working on another wavelength, passes along through the invisible until It finds another body in harmony with Its require-ments, as near Its own wavelength as possible. Soul enters into that body perhaps while it is still in the womb of its mother, or directly after birth.

Music is a wavelength, as is electricity, or any other particle in the specialized stream of Spirit. Remember the stories of how harmony can soothe the wild beasts and serpents. There are tales of holy men who live among the wild animals and are never both-ered; these same animals often attack those who try to harm the holy ones. Music, as a wave pattern, is often used as a way of adjusting the vibrations of the human mind and body which have lost rhythm and lack harmony.

As one becomes more and more capable of sur-vival, one passes beyond serenity into what is known as God Consciousness. He can see that colors have wavelengths. This explains why some colors are very annoying, and some are pleasant. Those that are annoying clash with the individual's wavelength, especially if he is less capable of meeting life's exigen-cies.

It has long been proven that music and colors go together. Color can further improve the effects of music upon a troubled mind. Disease, as you know, is a disharmony resulting from the influence of an imaged picture. Music could return the balance if necessary, but one would have to reach the basic cause in order to erase the image.

Even certain localities and cities have their own wavelengths established by the Souls dwelling there.

To live in surroundings where the wavelengths are compatible with your own makes for congenial surroundings, but to have to work in those where the vibrations are not at all in harmony will leave you nothing but unhappiness. Hence, one will harmonize his surroundings with his own wavelengths, either adjusting himself, or leaving. Unless this is done the individual will descend to misery.

This leads to still a greater truth; that the world itself vibrates on a certain wavelength, and is, in fact magnetic. No one will deny that the earth has magnetic poles called the North and South Poles. We also know that, owing to the composition of the strata of the earth's crust, different parts of the earth's surface are more magnetic than others, and throw out different wavelengths. It can be easily understood why one place suits one person more than another. Also, some people sleep better when the bed faces East-West than when it faces North-South and other directions.

All these are manifestations of an invisible force which sweeps this earth and the whole universe. As there is more iron ore and other conductive metals unevenly distributed below the earth's surface, so the magnetic vibrations will vary from point to point.

The power of thought itself is a vibration, a wavelength, and the sender can make it travel into the ether any distance by pure mental determination. Soul manifests in graduations of fineness, produced by vibrations.

Elements differ not in substance, but in rate of vibrations. A piece of ice changes into water and into steam, vapor and gas, not changing in its substance of H_2O, being still two atoms of hydrogen and one atom of oxygen, but by increasing the rapidity of its atomic and electronic vibrations.

This represents the spirit of truth, which leads you to all truth. Each must believe, or rather, have a certainty on what he knows; if the willingness to accept is in the individual, the power to recognize truth is also there. Therefore, one must start from the premise that he knows nothing. One must have certainty. This is the answer to all things.

Why is it so necessary to have certainty before you can enter into the life of all truth? Why? Because thought builds. Soul is part of the ECK, and cannot be divided. You, Soul and consciousness, contact the creative power provided you do not place other thoughts of doubt and fear in the way. What you image in your mind, when your thoughts are clearly of belief, attracts the creativeness of ECK. Consciousness images forth an outline, and this is filled with life. It lives. You do not doubt it. Thus you prepare an outline, a structure that is filled with life, and what you image comes to pass. Those who are cold and aloof make little progress, but the ones who are warmly responsive make swift, and often dramatic, progress. Why is this? It is because the wise ones put feeling into their thoughts about truth.

Belief must be a powerful conviction. You must feel strongly about it, then wonders pour into your life. You go forward to meet them.

The study of the scriptures is good but they do not give self-knowledge of absolute happiness; for books and scriptures simply remind us of the higher truths. They cannot bring the highest truth within our reach. The scriptures describe certain spiritual truths, such as the existence of God, divine love, and Spirit, but one cannot gain the realization of these truths from books anymore than he can squeeze a drop of water out of an almanac, in which the annual rainfall is mentioned. Then what does a person do to find truth?

There are several ways. Go to a person whom you know by evidence, knows the truth and ask to be taught, or set out on a course to find it by yourself. If you are strong enough in this quest you will find it.

The consciousness of the self, then, is that which we must know, in order to approach the Altar of Spirit and ask for permission to enter into Spirit, Itself. If we are free from negation, then Spirit will allow us to become a part of its Godly attributes and use us as the distributing channel, to produce forms in this world.

The body or mind itself has not the power to see or perceive any external object. By analyzing our perceptions we can understand that the activities of the sense organs are unconscious by nature. The conscious self illuminates the organic functions, and is the seer of sights, the hearer of sounds, and the knower of all sensations. It is also the thinker of thoughts within us. That intelligent self, which is the source of consciousness and knowledge, must be known as the director of the mind and senses. When we have realized the cause of self-consciousness, we have understood the power which directs Soul, mind, and body.

Soul, or consciousness, is a finer substance in vibration. The vibration of consciousness produces perceptions and sensations and reveals things which cannot be revealed by vibrations of grosser matter. The functions of consciousness are but vibrations of the finer particles of the ethereal substance called Sattva in Sanskrit; one of the parts of the great sound current of HU. It is not to be confused with the three gunas of Yoga and Vedanta philosophy—sattva, rajas, and tamas, which are the three qualities of mind.

139

The vibrations of this substance do not produce intelligence or consciousness. The mind appears as an intelligent being when it is in contact with Soul, just as a piece of iron having absorbed the heat of a furnace, appears as hot and able to burn. The conscious self may be compared to a magnet which attracts the iron of the mind substance. When a piece of iron being attracted by a magnet, moves, that motion is not natural with iron, but is caused by its proximity and close contact with the magnet. As the very presence of the magnet produces activity in the iron, so the very presence of Soul creates the activity of the mind substance, but Soul is not confined within the limits of the mind substance, because the true Soul is beyond all relations of space and time.

The true purpose of any seeker is to know Soul as his beingness. This leads into wisdom and one becomes immortal. Those who know that the source of intelligence is Soul, attain immortality; those who do not know it remain attached to the material body and senses and are therefore subject to birth and death. Become conscious of the immortal Soul. When this consciousness of the immortal self is gained, all fear vanishes. Fear of death rises from ignorance, which makes us forget our immortal nature and identify ourselves with the material body, which is subject to death.

Becoming one with the mortal body, we fear death and thus experience anxiety and misery. How can we expect to be free from the fear of death when we have identified Soul with the body, which will surely die? This fear, however, ceases to trouble anyone who has realized that the body is like a shell, a house, a receptacle of Soul, which is deathless by nature. The Soul manufactures the physical body, by Spirit, in order to fulfill certain desires and purposes of life. He who knows this truth has risen above all fear.

It is most difficult to realize the true purpose of life. Few persons in this world have found a perfect standard by which they can measure correctly, whether or not they have fulfilled that purpose. Each of us has to find out that the highest ideal of life is the attainment of that state in which one knowingly becomes a channel for ECK, and secondly, the attainment of self-knowledge.

This brings one to absolute freedom. It is by self-knowledge and becoming the channel that we can obtain everything we desire. The knowledge that is usually possessed is only a part of the all-knowing nature of the Divine Spirit. Imperfection is due to inherent limitations, the imperfect conditions of intellect which reflect the divine wisdom. When limitations are removed and the intellect is purified, true and perfect wisdom begins to shine within.

Knowledge is always one, not many. The same limited knowledge that we now possess will be the highest knowledge when it reveals the individual "I." Those, who know the divine Self, attain to immortality even during this lifetime.

We can now see that everything in the universe has its origin in idea, in thought, and it has its completion in the manifestation of thought through form. Many intermediate stages are necessary, but the cause and effect of the series are the thought and the thing. This shows that in essence the thing had already existed in thought. It is this general principle of "the already existence of the thing in thought" that we have to lay hold of. As we find this in an architect's design of a house that is to be, so we find it true in the great work of divine ECK. When we see this, we have realized a general principle at work everywhere. This is consciousness. If it is a true fact that the thing must be in thought before thought can form the thing, then it is plain that the divine ideal can only be externalized in our objective life to the proportion it is first formed in our thought. It takes form from our thoughts only to the extent we have apprehended its existence in the divine ECK.

By the intrinsic nature of the relation between the individual "I" and the divine ECK this becomes strictly a process of reflection and to the proportion the mirror of our consciousness blurs or clearly reflects the image of divine ideal, so there rises a correspondingly feeble or vigorous reproduction in our external life.

Now to the original point. Soul is the thinker of thoughts. The consciousness responds when directed by Soul, which is beyond all thought, beyond all matter, energy, space, and time. The very act of thinking imposes self-consciousness because all thoughts are possible only through self-consciousness. Therefore that which I am, that which is above and beyond all thoughts, cannot be revealed by the consciousness nor the intellect. Even when the consciousness cannot think of it, it is possible for Soul, which I am, to know the whole thing in a complete way.

This being true why should we limit our concept of the divine ideal of ourselves? You have shut your eyes to the fact that the divine effect of conception would be nothing but an illusion if it were not capable of expression in the outer world at large. In the creative process of Soul we become the individual reflection of what we realize the divine power to be, relative to one's self. If we realize the divine as the infinite potential of all that can constitute a perfect human being, this conception must, by the law of creativity,

142

gradually build up a corresponding image in our thoughts, which in turn will act on our external condition.

This, by the Law of Consciousness, is the nature of the process. What is required is to see more clearly the law of this sequence and use it intelligently. The fact, which, in our past experience was not grasped, is that the human consciousness forms a new point of departure for the work of the ECK. In proportion as one sees this more and more clearly, the more he shall himself enter into a new order of life in which he is less subject to the old limitations. There develops a deeper understanding of the supreme law of our being. We are dealing with the self-originating action of ECK. A new force has to be taken into account, the power of feeling. Thought creates form, but it is feeling that gives vitality to thought.

Thought without feeling may be constructive as in some engineering work, but it can never be creative in the work of an artist, or a musician. In all that which originates within itself a new order of causation needs to be recognized, a creation, the intertwined reality of thought and feeling. It is this inseparable union of thought and feeling that distinguishes creative thought from analytical thought and places it in a different category. If one is to utilize a new starting point for carrying on the work of creation it must be done by assimilating the feeling of the divine ECK into the pattern of one's thought, by entering into the stream of the ECK.

The images in the mind from the stream of Spirit have to be generic. The reason is that by its very nature the principle of life must be prolific, tending to multiplicity, and the original thought image must be fundamental to the whole race, not limited to particular individuals. Consequently the image in the stream of the ECK must be an absolute type containing the true essentials for the perfect development of the race, just what Plato meant by archetypal ideas. This is the perfect substance of the thing in thought.

Therefore, it is that our unfolding as centers of creative activity, as exponents of new laws, and through them of new conditions, depends on our realization that divine power is the archetype of consciousness perfection, at once as thought and feeling. There is nothing lacking here that one cannot understand by his senses. Since the very essence of cognition is that it dispenses with the physical presence, one finds himself in a position of communication with a being at once divine and human.

The original image is simply generic in itself, and it becomes active and specific by a pure personal relation of the individual. Once more we must realize that nothing can take place except through the channels of law, and the specific relation is not arbitrary, but must derive from universal laws under certain conditions. The ordinary laws of the world originate precisely from the fact that no law covers these certain conditions; it must follow that the specialization of the law must be provided by the individual. It is up to the individual. His recognition of the originating creative movement arises from a combination of thought and feeling, enables it to become a working tool. He is certain that there is a power outside and inside himself—which works with his consciousness and makes life warm, vivid, and full of interest.

Since specialization can only take place through the individual, it logically follows that the life which he thus specializes, becomes his own life. One comes to know that ECK will eventually reach the point where It doesn't recognize Itself apart from self and self's desires. Self-recognition through the individual cannot change the inherent nature of the creative Spirit, and therefore, to the extent to which the individual recognizes Its identification with himself, he places himself under Its guidance and becomes one who is led by It. He begins to experience the cause and effect of the supreme ideals in himself, in a small degree at first, but containing the principle of perpetual growth into infinite expansion.

A secret doctrine of ECK brings out these same principles. That the outer person with all its actions should not be held responsible, since it does not possess any degree of divine consciousness or spiritual illumination by which it can determine and decide what is right or wrong. It has no future, only a brief present moment of existence.

We find that truth tells us that the Spirit of God flows into and through us all, that if we cut ourselves off from one another, we cut ourselves off from the free flowing of Itself. Now there are found various types of people; the unresponsive, the difficult-to-convince, the independent who will not accept a free gift when offered lovingly, and those who find life rather hard. The responsive ones are the ones who make contact easily with God.

Responsiveness brings one to the realization that if we pride ourselves on being independent, refuse to be under obligation to others, expect no one to be friendly, no matter how much they are trying to prove they are, stand on our dignity, forget the childlike spirit that is taught, we put a block in our lives which not only keeps others away but keeps out God's blessings.

We must have truth in order to have power. Be truthful in your thoughts. Never shy away from a critical thought from a sense of mistaken kindness to yourself. Never make a deliberate effort to forget something unpleasant. It is our responsibility to face the things we have created.

Before you can give truth to others, truth must be known as the absolute need in your life. We must see truth and know truth and think truth always.

Refuse to see truth, pretend that it is impossible to know what is true and what is not, distort truth, seek to mix it with untruth, attempt to deceive both ourselves and others, give truth in an unattractive manner, then chaos will reign in our lives. Our real inner self will be in conflict with our outer self and we will continually find ourselves in the most unpleasant situations.

If we follow truth explicitly we will realize an awareness of that something within us, which is eternal and deathless, indestructible, calm and wise.

It is like that old saying, "let us think of ourselves as being safe within the circle of eternity, cradled like babes in the arms of the divine power until we have time to know It, time to grow and become conscious of being Its sons."

This is the time for truth "the truth, the whole truth and nothing but the truth." This is no time for half-truths, for bewilderment and lack of understanding. These constitute the soil in which grief grows. In truth alone is there comfort, understanding and courage.

Gradually we come to a complete understanding. We are eternal beings in the eternity of God. When we know the shape of the altar, understanding will come to us.

Look at the shape of the altar, it is your own consciousness.

146

10

The Records of Heroes

*I*n my research and travels I have found that spiritual giants are more numerous than can be imagined. Looking through the history of the religious records I find that the annals of the Orthodox Church alone contain more written records about its spiritual heroes than one could digest. This group is but a small segment of the whole—and out of the whole come thousands and perhaps millions of those who have travelled the higher path; teachers, reformers, savants, saints, avatars, munis, rishis, and white magicians, yet none can reach the high standard of the ECK Masters, those who belong to the Order of the Vairagi Adepts.

There are so many that I cannot see why man has been so stubborn in nature hanging on to the material world, thinking that his salvation lies here and now instead of in the higher realm. It is a wonder to all why man has continually been a slave to his outer self. Why he has let the tyrannical sway of the material world rule him through fear of such things as security. Even today, as throughout the history of this physical universe, we have the population of the world ruled by a small minority, or by a single individual. It all reverts back to the age-old adages, "Be the master or the slave," "Lead or be led," or "Exploit or be exploited." These have been mottoes of this world. But remember that no one is forcing the slave to remain the slave. If he is going to insist on being dominated, then there has to be the one who dominates, who does not join the herd. It is all a matter of choice.

It sums up to a secret. Stop needing; stop letting yourself be dominated. This is the secret—be independent of the things of this world, you will have them; turn your back on them and act the part, you will get help when you no longer need it. For there is another old adage "Heaven helps him who helps himself."

Think a little, and you will see that you have received what you seemed to need either through unconscious or positive behavior, through action rather than reaction, through inventiveness, rather than through negative motions. It amounts to this: Stop reacting and start making others react.

For example, put yourself in the position of needing money, and you are never going to get enough of it. Because you don't rule money, you are letting money rule you. Money is only a manifestation, a symbol of value that has an exchange value for goods—it is neither positive nor negative. It is only when you react to it that it becomes negative.

We all have the tendency to let ourselves become slaves. This is the herd instinct. We all have the tendency to want to follow some sort of leader, out of pure negative laziness; to let someone else do our thinking for us, and to take over our responsibilities. Actually, he will simply load us down with more of them. We want more worldly goods because we have acquired this habit—a purely negative habit, and we are too spineless to break the habit. Once the individual sets a price on himself, whether for his services or for his integrity, nobody will want him. Refuse to set a price and people will swarm on their knees to him because they know he can be trusted.

Money in itself is neither positive nor negative. It is simply a manifestation. Since we exist within material bodies on a material plane, we cannot escape manifestation. We affirm a thing by denying it, just as much as we do by accepting it. The correct attitude is to agree to its worth, but never need it. In this universe too steadfast a positive attitude is likely to bring an overwhelming reaction in others, perhaps even destruction. The trick is to give in occasionally, but always be able to walk away from the situation—never to need anything so badly that you cannot do without it.

From this brief discourse, you now know why most holy men usually are obscure, destitute by the material world standards, and are like hermits in their ascetic ways. Like certain priestly sects and Buddhist monks, they have reached the state where they no longer need anything. They are free of response.

There is a danger in learning the secret knowledge, and many of its teachers know this. It lies in the fact that many, who have become adepts in the art of communication, command, through the invisible power, for self purpose. They learn the art of using the two-edged sword, that truth can be used for both good and evil. Persons, who use the evil side of the art of truth, are known as black magicians and they can take control over life for the purpose of destruction. They can use the negative powers of this world for the purpose of destruction and often are hired for that reason, by unscrupulous individuals to better the latter's own end.

The individual who starts on the upward path must be careful how the inner powers are used. The divine ECK has a way of reversing Itself and punishing those who use It negatively, even causing the death of the user. Many of those who are believed to be spiritual giants are actually black magicians, and there is little need to give them any attention. Sometimes we awaken too late to find that we are under the power of someone who is subverting our desire to reach God, to become a channel of the divine ECK.

The seat of truth resides in the imagination, but is not actually in it. Do not let this paradox throw you. The imaginative faculty is also the seat of bewitchment. Once an idea takes hold it cannot be destroyed until another one replaces it in the opposite direction. The power of imagination of the mind is fantastic. If it is obsessed by love of Spirit, it can carry Soul into the higher planes; likewise if possessed by fear, it can bring about death.

Those who have a trained and powerful will can exercise a great deal of influence upon a passive and fearful person, even to the point of bringing about death. The basic law underlying all magical work and spiritual endeavor is that energy follows through. In the study of processes and rites to effect a magical operation we find that the power behind these operations is always the same, imagination controlled by a trained will, and directed toward a definite end. Incantations, repetitions or words of a particular sound-vibration, rhythmic movements and concentration of the attention on a symbol, a magnetically charged object, any and all these serve to generate a force which is discharged with overwhelming energy at the climax of the rite. Those who are true Masters have this force always at their disposal without recourse to such practices, for they have attained to the kingdom of power, which is the kingdom of heaven.

Whatever you hold in your mind is bound to come into existence sooner or later. The idea is the thing itself. It is affirmed that God has given to the sons of men the power to manifest ideas, to make them solid. Soul, being generated by Spirit, is the son, the offspring of the real man. Soul, when completely permeated by the life of Spirit, has power to originate forms in the outer world. This is clearly taught in a remarkable passage of the Shariyat-Ki-Sugmad, which contains a great truth and principle, "Whosoever shall find himself in Me, shall do good works. And who does desire to do good works and refuses to abide in Me shall suffer until he learns My law. For I am the tree on which you grow as the leaf and cannot become more than this unless you are obedient to My law."

At a later passage in the same book: "Unless you look into My heart, all thy seeking is for naught. When you do see what is there you are blessed."

It is an old doctrine, older than Plato, that ideas are real things. Real things belong to the unseen world, lie beyond the grasp of the senses. That which our eyes see is not the thing itself, but a phenomenon or appearance. We do not see the realities of our life with our physical eyes. To perceive the image of someone is to see the living idea of him. This is the real man, the spiritual entity, whom we love and reveals the true doctrine of platonic love, of which men speak without knowing what it means. Yaubl Sacabi said of the rabble, that having eyes, they saw not, and having ears, they heard not. The external is the apparent and phenomenal, the shadow and not the substance. If the spiritual idea of it is the real side of it, and if we can take this into ourselves and understand it, then we can cooperate with Spirit to be Its channel.

Emerson said, "The heart which abandons itself to

151

the Supreme Mind finds itself related to all its works, and will travel a royal road to particular knowledges and powers. When we have broken our god of tradition, and ceased from our god of rhetoric, then may God fire the heart with Its presence."

Every person is surrounded by an emanative sphere. This is represented by the aura, a nimbus seen around the heads of the saints and divinities in pictures. This is a circle or disc of rays invisible to our senses, but plainly perceptible to the inner vision. It is by no means a fantasy, but an actual part of the individual; an emanative sphere of our thoughts and feelings, of our own particular universe. It is different in different persons, and differs in the same person at different times, as it is always in correspondence with our inward states. The Living ECK Master often cures disease by purifying the atmosphere both within and without the person. He does this by the power of the inward word and the ECK, and by touch. All of us can do this, if we take the time to learn that we are agents of the divine ECK.

We, then, must be of this motto, "Living is the wish fulfilled." Each individual has free will to choose what he thinks, and what he thinks within comes forth visibly in his life without. It is like having a door opened, just by a stated truth. Sometimes the door by the stated Truth opens widely, just as some of you have experienced. We do not differ as human beings in the amount of power we have—our only difference is in the amount of power we realize that we have.

All adepts know that thought processes creative power. The whole superstructure depends on this foundation. This starting point—pure mental action—is the source from which existing creation comes into manifestation. We know that every manifestation is in some essence the expression of divine thought. The old metaphysicians broke this into three parts, (1) visualization, which produces prototypes; (2) meditation, which shows forth considerations; and (3) contemplation, which are postulates.

Therefore, you should find that your mind is an expression of divine thought. Divine thought produces something which itself is capable of thinking. But the question at hand brings us into wondering whether its thinking has the same creative quality as that of the divine ECK.

The whole of the creative process consists in the continual pressing forward of the divine ECK for expression through the individual and the particular, and the Spirit in Its different modes is the life and substance of the universe. There is an expression of thinking power which subsists latent in the divine ECK. If it were less than this it would only be some sort of mechanism and would not be thinking power. Thinking power must be identical in kind with divine ECK. It is for this reason that man is said to be created in the image and likeness of God. Once you realize this you find a firm foundation from which to draw many important pieces of intelligence.

At first you will not understand why you are hampered by adverse conditions, but then it will come to you that you are using your power invertedly. One usually takes the starting point of thought from external facts and consequently creates a repetition of facts of a similar nature, and so long as you do this, you will keep on repeating the old circle of limitation. This is merely because you are accepting responsibility caused by effect and it changes your flow, making an inflow instead of an outflow.

Owing to the sensitive reaction of the subconscious

mind to suggestion I find that one subjects himself to very powerful negative influences from those who are unacquainted with the positive principles, and thus race beliefs and thought currents of his environment tend to consolidate his inverted thinking.

Therefore, it is not surprising that the creative power of thought is used in the wrong direction producing the very limitations which one fights and complains about openly. The trouble is that he is the effect of the inflow of the world and his environment. So by reversing the flow to an outflow, and instead of taking his starting point from the external conditions, he takes the position of receiving it from the inward, Soul. He reaches a conclusion—determining great principles by simple deduction long before knowing anything about the teaching of truth; first, by realizing that the whole manifested cosmos could have its origin nowhere but in the divine power of man, and secondly, by realizing that his own self must be the same in kind as that of the divine power.

Lao-tzu, the spiritual hero of China said, "The world may be known without leaving the house. The way may be seen apart from the windows. The further you go, the less you will know. Accordingly, the wise man knows without going, sees without seeing, and does without doing." This means that the inner world of a man reflects the world around himself; the principles of both worlds are the same. Certainty is to be found only in the heart; confusion is bred in the outer world.

The point here is that one must have a definite idea of what one would achieve. As thoughts are creative, plan only those things that would be a blessing to all. If you don't, you may be creating something that will bring you the reverse of blessings.

154

St. Teresa said that the power of Soul can be perpetuated and intensified. By the very nature of the creative process the consciousness is itself a thought of the divine power. As long as thought of the divine ECK subsists, we will subsist, for we are in It. As long as we think this, It will continue to subsist for us in the postive manner, fulfilling the logical condition required for the perpetuation of the individual life. Remember that the potential infinitude of the individual is limitless. There is no limit of absorption. Once you have grasped the idea of your individuality as a thought in the divine ECK which is able to perpetuate itself by thinking of itself as the thought which it is, you have gotten to the root of the whole matter, and by the same method you will not only perpetuate your life, but will also expand it.

One then resolves that his own discoveries are the results of his seeking, and once he arrives at this conclusion, his understanding needs comparison with the reports of the mystics of all ages in other lands. It has been found that the remarkable unanimity of the great mystics of India, China, Persia, the Holy Lands, and Europe are one of the most impressive facts of the spiritual history of the human race. Furthermore, one will find that his own discoveries are in line with them. One will learn that this agreement among them is due to personal causes. They start with general skepticism about traditional religion and man's power to influence his gods or God. Their insight was derived from an overwhelming experience of a power, a reality beyond themselves. They discovered that the intellectual was clearly a by-product, rather than an object in itself, though they, themselves, were skilled thinkers.

Their own satisfaction came only with a sense of the divine reality, the Godhead, of a fountain of power that was back of the thinker, back of all apparent cause.

What is this Godhead, this reality, like? I will try to carefully explain it again. The first principle drawn is this: Reality, which is designated as one, is an all-embracing unity from which nothing can be separated. Jesus said, "The Lord our God is one Lord." Later Eckhart, of Germany, repeated this statement, "The likeness born of the ONE leads Soul to God, for he is One unbegotten unity." Kabir said, "Behold the One in all things." And the *Tao Te Ching* scriptures repeat, "Something there is, whose veiled creation was before the earth or sky began to be; silent, so aloof and so alone it changes not, nor fails, but touches all."

The second principle is this: It, the Ultimate is nameless, indescribable, beyond telling, and therefore anything said about It is faulty. Then what name does one give to It? God told Moses, "I am That I am." Sankara of India, said, "It is God's nature to be without a name. To think of His goodness, or wisdom, or power is to hide the essence of Him, to obscure it with thoughts about Him." Again Eckhart repeated, "Who is Jesus? He has no name."

The third principle is: Within the self, the ultimate is to be found and there is identity with reality in the external world. In the first book of the Bible the author says, "So God created man in his own image, in the image of God created he him." Jesus repeated, "The Father is in me, and I in him," and "I and my Father are one." Eckhart stated, "As sure as the Father, so single in nature, begets His son, begets him in the Spirit's inmost recess, there is the inner world. Here, the core of God is also my core; and the core of my Soul, the core of God's." One of the Indian Upanishads says, "In this body of yours, you do not receive the truth;

but there in fact it is in that which is the subtle essence, and you are that." Bayazid of Persia, "I went from God to God, until they cried from me, in me. O' thou I."

The fourth principle is: It can be known, not discursively, but by acquaintance, and this acquaintance is the point of all living things. Jesus said, "This is life eternal, that they might know thee the only true God." Ansari of Herat, "Know that when you learn to lose yourself, you will reach the Beloved. There is no other secret to be learnt, and more than this is not known to me." Eckhart, "Where is God in eternity? Nobody could ever find God. He has to discover himself. But when one takes God as he is Divine, he will be like one athirst; he cannot help drinking even though he thinks of other things."

The fifth principle is: Reality is disclosed only to those who meet its conditions and the conditions are primarily of an ethical nature. Jesus said, "Blessed are the pure in heart: for they shall see God." Eckhart reported, "The more a man regards everything as Divine—the more Divine that It is of Itself—the more God will be pleased with him. This requires effort and love, a careful cultivation of the spiritual life. One must learn an inner solitude. He must learn to penetrate things and find God there to get a strong impression of God fixed firmly in his mind." A Sufi sutra brings this out, "When the heart weeps for what it has lost, the Spirit laughs for what it has found." A Lanavantra Sutra says, "With the lamp of word and discrimination one can go beyond word and discrimination and enter the path of realization."

We have learned that we are a reflection of the Divine Spirit. All external conditions, including the body, are produced by thought. What is found along

157

with the five principles and conclusions of the ancient and modern mystics, is that we ourselves stand between two infinities, the infinity of Spirit and the infinity of substance. From both we can draw what we will and mold specific conditions out of the substance by the creative power which we take from the Divine Source. This is not the force of personal will upon the substance of divine power, an error that will land us in all sorts of inversions, but a realization of the consciousness as a channel through which the Divine Spirit operates upon substances in a particular way, according to the mode of thought which we are seeking to embody.

This is the explanation of the paradoxical expression in the Chinese mysticism of Wei Wu Wei. It sounds negative, yet it is a positive action; to do without doing, to act without action. To use a more familiar phrase, the idea is to let God be God in you. To live as the nature of things does. Jesus said, "Consider the lilies how they grow: they toil not, they spin not."

If, then, our thoughts are habitually concentrated upon the principles instead of particular things, realizing that principles are nothing more than divine power in operation, we shall find they will necessarily germinate to produce their own expression in corresponding facts, that will benefit us greatly. Jesus said to verify this, "Seek ye first the kingdom of God, and his righteousness; and all these things shall be added unto you."

We must never lose sight of the reason for the creative power of our thought. It exists because our consciousness itself is a thought form of our power. Our increase in livingness and creative power has to be in exact proportion to our perception of our relation to Spirit. This is the basic conception of the princes

158

with its culmination in the conception of heirs of the throne. These are not mere fancies but the expression of strictly scientific principles in their application to the deepest problems of individual life and their basis is that each person's world on any plane must necessarily be created by his own consciousness. In its turn, his mode of consciousness will necessarily take its color from his conception of his relation to the Divine.

One must have a love for God and humanity which underlies the wonder-working of miracles. Love is the unspoken word. Love for all with nonattachment will lend power to any properly directed channel, or distributing agency. The individual whose heart is wide open to God contacts a power above this physical expression. A lover of God taps sources of power and blessings completely unknown to the reserved and closed-in persons. It has been said that he who saves his life shall lose it, and he who loses his life for God, saves it. If you refuse to open your heart, trying to keep an interest in yourself and that of your immediate circle, you will lose all you value; if you open your heart and love all that you value most, you will win life. This is the divine law of the ages.

Now you can understand why the truly spiritual person works only for the betterment of those around him, and for all. He is wise to remain on the path to God, rather than slip off to the downward path of glory furnished by the powers for destruction. His clearest thought is: I will become an effect if I do not state positively what I intend to do.

The path is neither positive nor negative, but it is a movement of the consciousness, Soul. It is an effortless movement, but nonetheless a movement, like the annual rhythm of the seasons. Lao-Tzu put it this way: "I do not know its name; A name for it is 'Way';

159

pressed for designation, I call it Great. Great means outstanding, going out, far-reaching, return." This suggests the lines of force in a magnetic field. They go out one pole and return to the other.

In another verse he states: "The way itself is like something seen in a dream. In it are images, elusive, evading ones. In it are things like shadows in twilight. In it are essences, subtle but real, embedded in truth." The Divine Spirit is therefore not impersonal; to coin a word It is proto-personal. That is, pregnant like a mother, with men as well as things. It is One, and God is in It; It therefore involves personality.

The way not only gives to each thing its being or existence, but it also gives to each its appropriate dynamics. Its particular quality is the force of life's energy, and such a powerful force that the spiritual heroes with whom I have come in contact seem to change one with a glance, seem to change the order of flow of the individual from inflow to outflow. In order to obtain this virtue of the way, one must surrender himself to it; it will not come automatically. Though masculine, he must adopt the passivity of the feminine, and then switch again to the masculine surrendering to the opportunity, allowing the Divine to flow through him. It is a denial, a giving up, a permitting of power to outflow through the spirit body into the outer world.

Thus the explanation for denial is: disclaiming all connection with the lower, mortal self; taking up the cross or burden of one's mortality and following the power into immortality.

We find the higher states of consciousness, "Self-Consciousness" and "Spiritual Consciousness," synonymous in man. Both are connected with the higher emotions and higher thinking, which are the emotional and thinking processes of man seldom used. Though both are important, neither constitute the final surrender that man must go through; the breaking of that hard shell of externalism in order to enter into the true spirit. Strange as it may sound, when one breaks through and allows himself to become the real channel for the divine power, he has what is called objective knowledge. This is distinct from sense knowledge—it is the knowledge of the ECK using man as Its agent to distribute Its energies and intelligence in a world of physical form or on any plane where the individual Soul might be dwelling independent of the body.

Spiritual development must be balanced in order to make an inspiring, happy and useful experience in the physical body. To provide this, the spiritual travelers, the Masters, found that there must be practice of the spiritual principles in this world which lead to happiness, livingness, kindness, tolerance, lovingness, and success.

Without the test of material results, there is the danger of the spiritual becoming a romantic emotion, unable to stand up to the stress of ordinary life. We should make full use of our spiritual development, of our faith on both the spiritual and physical levels. In this way we safeguard ourselves against the lack of balance and become a source of benefit and inspiration to others.

Not only is the ECK able to demonstrate that we need to balance the three parts of man's self, physical, Soul and Spirit, but many others have clearly done this. St. Andrew Fournet, a priest of the Catholic Church, was witnessed in 1824, to have blessed two small heaps of barley grain, hardly twenty bushels, and the good sisters of his retreat drew from them for three months without the supply showing any signs of diminishing.

At another time he multiplied ten bushels of corn into no less than sixty bushels. Later he multiplied money for the parish when it had to make payment on an immediate debt. Just enough and no more. St. John Bosco, of Italy, multiplied fifteen rolls to feed a number of boys in his parish in 1860. Mother Superior Pelleter, through the intervention of St. Germaine, deceased, fed 116 starving people, by miracles. There are many more famous examples given in the record of spiritual heroes; however, we must turn again to the study of the cosmic power.

We must accept this principle of the divine power. It is not a question of expecting to have—that which we desire is already waiting. This is the operation of the power. God's abundance is hidden in the creative, invisible substance, which contains all things. The power does not wait for us to ask it to prove what wonders it can perform, for we already know. What we want is for the wonders to be performed. It is this: when we ask in a believing way we are contacting the creative, invisible substance with our consciousness and shaping it into what we need. When we are afraid to expect too much, we don't ask; so the creative substance is not shaped by our thoughts, and we don't get it. We find all sorts of queer excuses, such as, God is angry with us, God is testing our faith, the time has not yet come, God favors some people and not others, or that the work we are doing is not important enough to warrant God's help. These reasons are most illogical, because if you look around, you will see that some very good causes rarely seem to get enough funds for support and many of them with very low ideals seem to prosper.

We also see that people with very holy aims some-times seem to be thwarted at all points, while others with exceedingly great faith in lucky charms seem to be most successful. The logical explanation and a very true one, is that the people who shape the invisible, creative substance with their directed thought power get results. Of course, people with low aims eventually learn that it was not worth it after all because they had sown poor seeds and finally reap a poor har-vest, either in this life or the next. All of us have the power to shape with our consciousness the creative substance, and the sooner we find this out and believe in it, the quicker shall we start living the abundant life. "Ye ask and receive not because ye ask amiss," says the scriptures. Starting now, ask in the right way, and receive.

There is always an earthly war of the material self conflicting with Spirit, until you learn how to take charge. The earth nature seeks to draw down, to desire its own comfort irrespective of what it should do; while the divine nature of man, the Soul-self, strives to overcome this lower nature, to lift it to the highest peak of capability. The sword of the divine Self in every man, though drastic at times, is healthy and altogether lovely. It lifts man eventually to unimag-inable heights of glory, power and splendor. All spiri-tual travelers, Masters, and saints feel the pull of the earth self which seeks its own comfort and safety, yet when they pray they are merged with the promptings of the Divine Power. The Father's will is the will of the highest, leading to untold bliss, not only in Heaven but now.

Why is it hard for a rich man to enter into the kingdom of heaven? This has puzzled man through the ages, ever since Jesus told the rich young man to sell his goods and follow Him. If a man is rich in consciousness of money for its own sake, and fails to seek the narrow door within himself which will lead to spiritual realization and spiritual powers; if he is wrapped in thoughts of gold, he cannot enter into the kingdom within. If a man is rich in the consciousness of intellectual gain for its own sake, he is just as handicapped. If he is rich in the consciousness of personal vanity, the same will happen to him. When the consciousness is locked in the realization of the kingdom within, as the outer world, it becomes as hard to enter as it is for a camel to go through the eye of a needle.

The proof and existence of the power lies in prayer itself. This helps to change the consciousness. The power knows but if it acts separately, intervening in the world's affairs directly without the cooperation of others, then prayer has little meaning and no logic.

We can rest in the knowledge that we, as heirs to the throne, are co-conscious workers with God, while on this Earth, for we are the divine distributors of Its power. We have the authority to draw down and concentrate the power, by prayer. All who need help and call on the power may open the inner door of the heart and receive the concentrated grace of God. It is never forced on anyone; they must ask and be willing to receive.

11

The Veil of Adonis

The veil of Adonis is an age-old mystery cult that arises from the legend of an ancient hero in the antiquity of time. It represents life, death, and resurrection and keeps the secrets of the cosmic spiritual power from the eyes of the profane.

It can be seen from a comparison of the ancient mystery rituals that the great themes, the ageless archetypes and their operation on Soul remain the same. The epic of the slain and resurrected Adonis was understood by those along the eastern shore of the Mediterranean Sea to signify "him of the double door," who survived the awesome miracle of the second birth, as Jesus did for the Christians.

We know that the legends and mystic rituals, in celebration of the god, associated with the renewal of vegetation, renewal of the moon, renewal of the sun, renewal of Soul, and solemnized at the resurrection of the year at springtime represented the ritual beginning of the Adonis legend. Throughout the ancient worlds such myths and rites abounded: the deaths and resurrections of Tammuz, Adonis, Mithra, Virbius, Attis, and Osiris. Even today we have the popular carnival games throughout the world which celebrate the deaths and resurrections of certain gods and saviors. We also have rituals concerning the fall and redemption, crucifixion and resurrection, the second birth of baptism, and the symbolic eating of flesh and drinking of blood.

Adonis, a beautiful young man who was in love with Venus, was killed by a wild boar. She sprinkled his blood upon the earth and flowers grew there. Her love was so great that she pleaded with her father, Zeus, the king of heaven to bring Adonis back from Hades, the nether world, but Persephone also laid claim to the handsome youth; so Zeus allotted his time beween the two goddesses. He was supposed to die during the late fall and be resurrected again in the spring. He was worshiped by the Greeks, Syrians, Egyptians, Babylonians, and the people of Cyprus, under various names, but the legend was the same.

In some cases Adonis was the sun god, who pursued Venus across the heavens. In other lands he was the morning star, with Astarte, the divine mistress, who was the evening star. In any case he is known to all as the lover of Aphrodite, goddess of love, embodiment of the lower energies of man and nature. Our interests in this are that he symbolizes the masculine, and Venus, the feminine qualities of the Divine Spirit. We find references to masculine and feminine qualities of Spirit in the teachings of the scripture and philosophies of all lands and people, but hardly anyone today teaches these combined qualities.

The old Chinese philosophers knew that the Cosmic Spirit contained both elements, at least in the material worlds. They tell us that the female characteristic is to withdraw. It is like a gateway through which man attains heaven, and heaven reaches man when he is receptive to its nature and open to its influence. Attaining, he can then go forth in the world and make use of its power through his masculine traits. To be open and receptive to the Spirit is to be useful without working at it. This is the law of this universe relating to living in a physical body.

Spirit appears in two ways in this world, the cosmic and the individual. Its essence is the same in both, but in each it works from a different angle. It is always the principle of Being; that which is, as distinguished from that which is not. But to grasp the true significance of this statement we must understand what is meant by "that which is not." It is that which, both is and is not at the same time, and the thing that answers to this description is "conditions."

The Spirit does this by the same method as in the original creation, namely, by creating something out of nothing. Otherwise it would be bound by the limitations necessarily inherent in the cosmic form of things, and so no new, fresh, creative starting point would have been attained. This is why most religions stress the theory of monism, of creation from a single power, instead of two. For this reason we have been told that the Oneness of Spirit is the foundation of all commandments, and that the Son of God is declared to be One-begotten.

The immense importance of this principle of creation from a single power becomes more apparent as we realize more fully the results proceeding from the assumption of the opposite principle, the dualistic aspect of the creative power. Here we will only say that the law of the reactive mind is the law of this universe, or in other words, the negative side of the many of his own making.

I offer no contradictions in speaking of the masculine and feminine nature of man for the mystery of

167

Adonis was to prove that instead of a twin power there was only the singular power which looked like a masculine power only. The singleness of the creative power is based on a knowledge that goes to the very roots of esoteric principles, and is, therefore, not to be set aside in favor of dualistic systems.

If it is possible to put the cosmic principle into words, it is that God is One, and that this "one" finds a center in ourselves, which means the result will center in ourselves, which in turn means the result will be new creation in and from ourselves. We shall realize in ourselves the working of a principle whose distinguished feature is its simplicity. It is Oneness and is not troubled by a dualness. To clear a point here—the trouble comes in the consciousness of the individual, not in the Spirit. We ought not contemplate how its action will be modified by that of some second principle, something which will compel it to work in a particular manner and so limit it, but rather we ought to contemplate its own Unity. Then we will see that its unity consists in a greater and lesser movement, just as the rotation of the earth on its axis does not interfere with its rotation around the sun; both are motions of the same unit, and are definitely related to each other. Likewise, we find that the Spirit is moving simultaneously in the macrocosm of the universe and in the microcosm of the individual, and the movement of the two harmonize because they are that of the same Spirit.

The great principle is the perception that the "I AM" is One, always in harmony with itself, including all things in this harmony for the simple reason that there is no second creative power. When the individual realizes that this "always singular power" is the root of his own being, and he has it centered in himself, and allows it to find expression through him, he learns to trust its singleness and the consequent harmony of its action in him with what it is doing around him.

Then he sees that the truth of Lai Tsi's "I am with God," is a necessary deduction from the correct understanding of the fundamental principles of being. Working on the principle then that the lesser must be included in the greater, one will desire that harmonious unity of action be maintained by the adaptation of his own particular movement to the larger movement of spirit working as the creative principle through the whole. In this way we become the distributing agents through which the God power finds specialization by the development of the personal factor on which the specific application of general laws must always depend. A specific sort of individuality is formed, capable of being linked between the great spiritual power and the manifestation of the relative in time and space because it consciously partakes of both. Also, because the individual has reached a plateau that recognizes the singleness of the spirit, as the starting point of all things, he endeavors to withdraw his mind from all arguments derived from external conditions, whether past or present, and to fix it upon the progress, the forwarding movement of spirit which he knows to be identical both in the universe and himself. He ceases the attempt to dictate to the spirit, because he does not see in it a mere blind force, but reveres it as the supreme intelligence. On the other hand, he does not kneel before it in fear or doubt because he knows it is one with himself, and is realizing itself through him. It cannot have any purpose antagonistic to his own individual welfare.

A man like this cannot fail. Spirit will honor his faith simply because it is eternal, unchangeable divine law. The two great errors that men make are: 1. Thinking that God, the Divine Spirit, is a being far away who listens or does not listen to the prayers of His children, according to His whim. 2. That Spirit which made the world is less powerful than the world It made. It is a case of choosing whether we will accept the world's law or Spirit law. Although we are living in the world, Spirit is living in us.

Faith then is perpetually in the present tense— when it asks, it mentally creates a mold and begins to draw magnetically the life to fill that mold and makes it appear in the visible world. This is man's relationship to God as the distributor.

In this way the individual becomes a center through which the creative force operates. Realizing this, he puts his thoughts deliberately under the guidance of the Divine Spirit knowing that his outward acts and conditions must thereby be brought into harmony with the great forward movement of Spirit, not only at the stage he has now reached but at all future stages. He doesn't deny his own thoughts as the creative agent in his own personal world: on the contrary, it is exactly on the knowledge of this fact, that his perception of the true adjustment between the principles of life is based. For this reason he feels that it is best to be led by that wisdom which can see what he cannot see, so that his personal control over the conditions of his own life may be directed to its continual increase and development.

In this manner the self ceases to be the petulant assertion of limited personality and becomes that which is the greater Self, affirming its own I-ness in the individual and through the individual. We become the vehicle for its expression and realize our true place as subordinate creative agents, perfectly independent of existing conditions because the creative method is monistic. It requires no other factor than Spirit, but at the same time a subordination to Spirit in the greatness of its inherent forward movement.

We see there is only one Spirit and it cannot antagonize various centers simultaneously. Spirit makes us the princes of the great King living in obedience to that power which has control and charge of our lives.

Spirit started flowing at the beginning of this universe and It flows still. It is for all who contact and keep It in mind. Belief of Its existence is the only possible way to contact It, since belief opens the thoughts to the Divine flow. If a man has doubted it deeply for years, it will be harder to cast away the doubts and re-educate the mind to belief. Not because truth of Divine Spirit is difficult to understand, but because it is so simple that the doubt-fettered consciousness cannot be still without being trained and guided to do so.

If this point is clear, then we are able to reach the next step, which is sincerity. If you have been an insincere person, believing easily what you wanted to believe, and conveniently forgetting what you did not want to believe; if you have loved flattery, if you have posed before others and tried to give a different impression of yourself than what you really are, then you will have no success in contacting Divine Spirit. Why is this? It is because we have sent down into the realm of the true, Soul-self so many lies that the Soul turns a deaf ear to us. When you try to get Spirit to answer prayers, it is unmoved, for it has learned there is a deep gulf between the center of truth within, and the untruthful outer self. If you have been an insincere person, then, you must long to be sincere. You must

171

make contact again with the true self—Soul—by thinking thoughts and saying words you know are true. An individual who is true to himself is a powerful person for all of his nature works together.

Whatever it is, you can have it. Assume that you have it, and go on pretending until it is yours. This can even apply to union of self with Spirit, but one must be childlike in nature, if he attempts this. You have to choose a quiet place where you can be alone, close your eyes and assume that you have already entered into the conditions and circumstances that you want in life. Make a real task of this, really feel the way it would be if you were in these conditions; see in your mind's eye all the details in a clear picture.

As children of God, we have a right to the riches of our Father. Children naturally inherit, and if Spirit does not pass on its riches to us, then who else is there to receive? Assumption has other meanings beside the usually accepted one. It means to make claim to a right or title. For by assuming one conceives an image in his mind and in the unseen world. When anything is conceived birth follows. Naturally that which has been conceived in the unseen world comes to birth in the seen, the visible world. Man's thoughts are creative of everything; whether they be happy or sad thoughts, good or evil thoughts, they create something that appears in the visible. Jesus simply said, "Ask, and ye shall receive, that your joy may be full," and "What things soever ye desire, when ye pray, believe that ye receive them, and ye shall have them."

The fulfilling of anything is the bringing into complete realization all that it potentially contains, and so the filling of any law to its fullness means bringing out all the possibilities which may be hidden in it. The complete manifestation of the law of indi-

172

viduality is the end to which the saints have striven, that which the legend of Adonis portrays. For once we are certain that God Is, we will be convinced that God is love, that a great power surrounds us in enfolded wings of tenderness, beauty and understanding. It is an ever-present, all-wise, intelligence interpenetrating all things, loving and supporting us all. When you are inclined to lose sight of this, you can say quietly within, "In Him I live, and move, and have my being."

Most of us are around people constantly who have tension, fear, headaches, deafness, rheumatism, illnesses, reserve and unwillingness to accept others as friends, heart troubles, timidity, and reluctance to face the world. These things, too, are sometimes interchangeable, so that one with heart defects may be reserved, a rheumatic person fearful, etc. The problem here is simply tension.

What causes tension? It is really fear. The tense person holds himself at bay, as though the world, everybody and everything in it, are vicious animals ready to devour him. What can overcome this? Belief in Spirit can take care of all things in the outer life. Life can become so relaxed, that it is a joyous possession. Many millions trust in Spirit and find the fulfillment of all their dreams.

This is based upon the spiritual and physical law that no effect can be produced except by the operation of an adequate cause. The Spirit is set before us explaining the causes and exhibiting the full measure of the effects. This is according to the action of Spirit and the importance of its universality and potential being inherent in all. There is no special law for anyone, but anyone can specialize the law by using it with a fuller understanding of how much can be gained from it. It is always there; it is always brought into greater existence by the individual and is, therefore, always ready, by its own inherent self, to continue creation from the individual consciousness as the necessary conditions are provided. Such conditions of course are thought conditions.

It is by the realization of consciousness of Spirit that one does receive a standard of thought which is bound to act creatively to bring out all the potentialities of our hidden being. The relation of pure consciousness of the Spirit is as the archetype idea in the all-creating Spirit. Here we arrive at the purity of consciousness as a concept of being, a universal principle, and as being; an idea capable of production in the individual Soul as the illumination of self. It is rather by the absence of individualistic endeavors that it produces the realization in external actuality of a purely conscious state. The best way to arrive at this is in the contemplation of the existing cosmos, and then transferring the conception of the Oneness of the power of Spirit from the cosmic, to the individual self, realizing that the same Spirit is able to do the same within ourselves.

The principle of the resurrection, as in that of Adonis, and the other high Souls, is the realization that man, by his individualization of Spirit, and his recognition of the fact that, since Spirit is always the same, he becomes the origin of a new creation from his own center of being.

All this is necessarily an interior process which takes place in the consciousness, but if we realize that the creative process is always primarily one of the involution-formation in the spiritual world, we see that the concentration of universal Spirit in the terms of personality on the spiritual plane happens to the individual who affords the necessary thought conditions.

Anyone who can understand this will discover that in Divine Spirit is present a divine individuality attuned to each individual person. It takes matters out of the region of intellectual speculation, which is never creative but only analytical and transfers it to the region of feeling and spiritual sensation which is the abode of the creative force.

Because Spirit is fundamental, we should trace from the start the creative processes of new thoughts which are personal to the individual, and which are repetitive at each higher level. The subsequent evolution of substance will mold new forms, continually increasing in agreement with Spirit and serving as vehicles for Spirit. Our starting point then is that of an ordained security from which we may quietly grow into the higher self which is the fulfillment of the law of our own being.

Man's great mistake is in the supposition that life can be generated in himself by an intellectual process. Intellectual knowledge is exceedingly important and useful, but its place in the order of the whole is not that of the originator, the Divine Spirit. Intellect is not life in itself, but a function of life; it is an effect and not the cause. Intellect is the study of the various laws arising from the different relations of things to one another. Consequently, it does not start from the true creative standpoint, that of creating something entirely new, or constructive.

To recognize negativism as a force of creation is to give up the creative standpoint altogether. It is to quit the plane of the first cause and descend into the realm of secondary causation and lose ourselves amid the confusion of a multiplicity of relative causes and effects without grasping any unifying principle behind it.

175

The only thing that can release the individual from the multiplicity of confusion is the realization of an underlying unity, and at the back of all things of the presence of one great positive principle without which nothing would have existence. We need not go beyond this single power for the production of anything. Consequently, if we look upon negativism as a force to be reckoned with, and therefore requiring study, we are in effect creating it. While on the other hand, if we realize there is only one force to be considered which is absolutely good, we are by law of the creative Spirit bringing that good into manifestation.

If you are following this you will know that we have now gone beyond cause and effect, into the Spirit of HU, the unknown creative force. We are in the area of the basic conception that there is a single originating power which is absolutely good and life giving, which penetrates all worlds. This is the graduating class moving into post-graduate work.

If ever there was a self-originating power which was destructive, then no creation could have come into existence, for the positive and the negative self-originating powers would cancel each other, and the result would be nothing. That which is called positive and negative would be the maya, the illusion which we have put there through imagination. Graduating, we do not have to study either any further, for the simple reason that it only requires our thoughts to be fixed on the good which we intend to create.

The reason for this is that every new creation carries its own law with it and by that law produces new conditions of its own. The Law of Spirit is never altered, but we have previously known it under limiting conditions. These conditions, however, are no part of the law itself. A clearer realization of this law shows us that it contains in itself the power of transcending all conditions. The law, which every new creation carries with it, is not a contradiction of the old law but its specialization for a higher manner of action.

Now the supreme principle of this Law of Spirit is that the production of life by the movement of Spirit in itself is necessary. All subordinate laws are merely the measurement of relations which spontaneously arise between different things when they are brought into manifestation. If an entirely new thing is created it must establish entirely new relations and so produce new sets of laws and new sets of circumstances. This is why we take the action of pure unmanifested Spirit as our starting point, we may trust it to produce manifestations of the law which, though perfectly new from our past experience, are quite natural in their own way as any that have gone before.

We see that the root of life is not to be found in the comparison of good and evil, but in the simple knowing that Spirit is the all creating power of that which is good. By trusting the Spirit to start a fresh operation in our consciousness, it will follow the law of its own being in the creation of the whole.

The only point to make here is that we must not forget that it is working through our own minds. It thinks through our mind, and our mind must be a suitable channel for its mode of operation by conforming to its broad lines of thinking. Divine Spirit can never change its essential nature as the crux of life and love. If we develop these two characteristics, which constitute the Law of Spirit, as the basis of our thinking, and reject all that is contrary to them, then we afford the general generic conditions for the specialized thinking of Spirit through our own minds. The consciousness, which is all the time being formed in ourselves, represents the basic factor of our spiritual life.

It is not a case of control by an external individuality, but the fuller expression of the Spirit through an organized consciousness which has, all along, been a less perfect expression of the Spirit, and the process of that growth.

You must understand that the individual is not losing his individuality when he works along these lines, but unfolds into fuller possession of himself by the conscious recognition of his personal share in the great work of creation. We grow into this new process from the very principle of life itself. The old thoughts based upon the comparison of limited facts, are now gone and are replaced with a new view and comprehension of principles.

We can move steadily upward. We know the certainty of the creative principle through which we work, which is working through us, and that our life, in its minutest details, is a harmony of expression. It is the paradox of the less containing the greater. We soon know exactly what we want to do and why we want to do it, and so we will act in a reasonable and intelligent manner. Gradually we shall see the greater thought which prompts our smaller one, and find ourselves working along its lines, guided by the invisible hand of creative spirit into continually increasing degrees of livingness which we need assign no limits, for it is the expansion of the infinite within ourselves.

In a sense Soul is esoterically neutral in its relation to the Divine Spirit, because its function is that of being receptive and formative. This is necessarily inherent because of the nature of the spirit's outward flow. Yet the individual's development as the specialization medium of Divine Spirit will depend entirely on his own conception of his relation to this essence of God. As the true nature of the relation between the individual consciousness and Divine Spirit becomes clearer to us, we find it to be one of mutual action and reaction, a perfect reciprocity. Eventually all is done from an act of goodwill, in complete confidence on both sides, and both are equally indispensable to each other. It is simply carrying out the principle that Spirit cannot act on the plane of the physical particular, except through the human channel via Soul.

A special relation becomes established between Spirit and the individual Soul, one of absolute confidence and personal feelings. There is no change in the Law of Spirit, but this is due to that specialization of its essence through the presentation of special conditions personal to the individual. Actually the changes that come about are in the mental attitude of the individual who has come into a clearer perception of God.

Thus, we come to the true meaning of the marriage of Adonis and Aphrodite; namely, the realization of the true relationship between Spirit and the individual consciousness. This is known esoterically as the mystical marriage in which the two have ceased to be separate and have become one. They have always been one, of course, but since we have hitherto comprehended things from the standpoint of worldly consciousness that makes it a practical reality for ourselves.

It is our conscious being which is the whole in which we wish to live. Whatever we draw from the Divine Spirit acquires in us the quality of beingness. This is why Spirit in relation to ourselves must necessarily assume a personal aspect, and why that aspect

179

which it will assume will be in exact relation with our conception of it.

We must enjoy the state of a calm and untroubled mind, in order for spirit to use us as a channel. This state can be reached by passing beyond the range of the happenings of the moment and this can be done by the discovery of our immediate relationship to the source of all good. This source is pure and undifferentiated. In these two words lies the secret of the whole position of our relationship with God. If we did not draw immediately from the Divine Spirit, our receiving would be subject to the limitations of the channel through which it reaches the external. If the force which we receive was not undifferentiated in itself then it could not take form in our minds and become to each individual just what we shape it to be.

We learn that Soul, of itself, is but an image and reflection of the infinite and has the power to differentiate limitlessly from the Infinite, the source of all things. A clear-cut recognition of the cosmic creative process shows that it cannot be anything else, and we find that it must possess this power, and that in fact it is our possession of this spiritual force which is the whole reason and mode of the creative process. In other words it is this; the power knows itself, and herein lies the whole secret of all things past, present and future.

Self-recognition, the self-contemplation of Spirit is the primary movement out of which all creativeness proceeds, and at attainment in the individual of a fresh center for recognition is what Spirit gains in the process. When the individual perceives this relation between himself and Infinite Spirit, he finds that he has raised from a position of slavery to one of reciprocity. Spirit cannot do without him any more than he can do without Spirit. Spirit is the unlimited essence of love, wisdom and power, all "three in one," undifferentiated, all waiting to be differentiated by the individual claiming to be the channel of their differentiation. The only requirement is for the claim to be made by the recognition of our very being. It is bound to be answered and with the right feeling, right seeing and right working for the particular matter we have in hand, it will flow in quite naturally.

The creative level is where new laws begin to manifest themselves in a new order of conditions, something transcending our past experience and thus bringing about a real advance. From this standpoint we may say that, as the individual wakes up to the oneness with Spirit, Spirit wakes up to the same thing. It becomes conscious of itself through the consciousness of the individual, and is absolved from the paradox of individual self-recognition by Spirit, without which no creative power could be possible. However, the Soul consciousness has to reach the level which provides the conditions for the arousing of the spirit to self-recognition in the individual.

It is spontaneous or nothing. This is why the Bible speaks of it as the free gift of God. It is self-responsibility, for it cannot be anything different. One does not originate the Spirit, but one originates himself, and he can do what he can do to distribute Spirit. The error of any friction is within man himself since God never changes. If you are limiting Spirit in some way, set about to find what it is. You are tying It down to conditions somewhat like saying It is hindered by reason of some existing form. The remedy is to go back to the original starting point of the cosmic creation and ask where were the preexisting forms that dictated to Spirit then. You may not get the answer now, but it will come in time. We must pass over all existing conditions, however adverse they may seem to be, and go straight to Spirit as the forming Spirit of new forms and new conditions. Spirit never changes, It is still the same, and is independent of existing conditions. When we do this, just trusting Spirit, and not laying down the particular details of its action, just telling It what we want, without dictating, we find daily that things will open more clearly both on the inner and outer planes.

Spirit is alive and working here and now, for if Spirit is to get from the past into the future it must be by passing through the present. What we have to do is to acquire the habit of living direct from Spirit in present time. This is a matter of personal relationship, perfectly natural and not requiring any abnormal conditions for its manifestation.

This was the relation of Aphrodite to Adonis, and is that worship in Spirit and in truth. The whole world is the temple of Spirit and you, yourself, are Its sanctuary.

Form is always the expression of Spirit, and since we are in touch with the forwarding movement of Spirit, we know that we, ourselves, will always be harmoniously included in any form of development which the great movement may take. Now, we advance our thoughts into another area of study of Spirit.

We have seen that the first stage in the creative process is feeling, the reaching out by Spirit in a particular direction. We may look for something of the same kind in the development of mankind and the great principles which we now know. History reiterates this point constantly. We can follow the movement of the race forward through feeling and thought to the present, where we have reached the apex of a culture which, so far as we know, has never been surpassed. Whether the process be individual or national it is always the same, the translation to the very highest plane—that of the Spirit force Itself—which brings about the old saying "Nature obeys us exactly in proportion as we first obey nature."

The forming Spirit of God is the life and the substance in each individual, here and now. It is the true parent of the individual both in body and Soul, just as It was in the original of all things. Human parentage is relatively unimportant, it is only the channel through which Divine Spirit has acted for the concentration of an individual center; the ultimate cause of that center, both in life and substance, continues to be the same One originating Spirit at every moment.

When we look at this and realize that Spirit is finding Its own individuality in us in Its twofold essence as life and substance, we see that It must be able and willing to create for us all good. The only limit is that which we, ourselves, impose by denying Its operation, and when we realize the inherent creativeness of Spirit we find that there is no reason why we should stop short at any point and say that it can go no further. The error is in looking on the life of the body as separate from the life of Spirit. Substance must emanate from Spirit and is nothing else than the record of the Spirit's conception of Itself finding expression in space and time. When we realize the true nature of the creativity of life, we learn that exterior things are changed by a change of the interior spiritual attitude. Our spiritual attitude is determined by our conception of our relation to infinite Spirit. When we begin to see that this relation is one of absolute reciprocity, the self-recognition of infinite Spirit, we find that the whole problem of life is solved in the simple balance of the all-creating Spirit as consciously identifying Itself with us. It has awakened to a new way of self-recognition peculiar to each of us, in which we individually form the center of Its creative energy. To recognize this is to specialize the principle of Spirit.

The originating movement of Spirit, from which all creation flows, can only be self-contemplation. Since Spirit cannot change Its nature, Its self-contemplation through our consciousness must be as creative in, for, and through us, as It was in the beginning. Consequently, we find the original creative process repeated in ourselves and directed by the conscious thought of our own minds.

There is no consideration of outward conditions, whether body or circumstances, for they are only effects not causes. Instead, we use the method of self-contemplation, knowing it to be the creative mood. We contemplate ourselves as allied to the infinite love and wisdom of the Divine Spirit, which will take form through our conscious thought, and act creatively, as a special providence entirely devoted to guarding, guiding, providing for and illuminating us.

The principle is love; when we are reunited to the Spirit in mutual confidence and love, what room is there on either side for any remembrance of our yesterday of sorrow?

When we have passed through the Veil of Adonis into the originating Spirit we are at one with the infinite. We act as the source of Its perfect works upon this plane of the universe.

12

The Borders of Heaven

hroughout this study we have been verging on the borders of the unknown, that which we call heaven, but heaven is only the invisible, the plane of the unseen. Many have stepped into this plane and lived by its laws, or great law, while still operating a body here in the physical universe. It is simple, but most people do not know or understand for they are really overlooking the subtle and seeing only the outer circumstances of life.

The science of thought is not a static science for it grows, and it grows through the individual. As his consciousness becomes greater to accept the Spirit which uses him as a distribution center for forming the forms of life, he gradually becomes Spirit, Itself. In time, he learns to trust It as much as It comes to trust him, and then, mutually, both are copartners in life. He, then, has passed the borders of that which has held him back from going into the realm of heaven. This border is often called the threshold.

Crossing the threshold of heaven can often be a terrible experience for the individual. He can see what heaven has to offer but cannot turn loose the outer in order to go into the bliss of life. He may even stay in this position for years quaking with terror at what might happen to him, if he should turn loose the outer, but desiring the inner plane so greatly that a constant war goes on within himself. This war between the little self and the Spirit has devastating effects upon the body, but once engaged, the Spirit will not let go, and will finally win out.

Very strangely, it is something which the individual has created for himself. He might ask himself this question: "What have I created for which I will not be responsible?"

Here lies the key. Those who are unable to let Spirit take over and handle their lives are living under the illusion of fear, anxiety, and distrust. They will not trust Spirit to take over their life and manage it for the good of the whole. These are the class of people who will not believe in miracles even though greater miracles take place in this day than during the times of Jesus. Today, more and more people are becoming acquainted with the laws of Spirit and are dwelling therein and recognizing that the Spirit of God is in each and all. What is needed is a strong desire, a banishing of doubt by an infusion of faith, a control and direction of thought, and a willingness to live a disciplined well-balanced life, unaffected by setbacks.

A logical thinker, as modern society knows him, is too often a poor candidate as an operative distributor for the Divine Spirit. Generally, they are not wise to the two main functions of life: First, God as Spirit is eternal, everywhere and unchanging; second, prayers by the millions have been answered down through the ages. What has been true of God, in the past, is true now; if true for some, it is true for all. The critical faculty has been the trouble; they have let it develop faster than their God faculty, which is the trusting childlike nature which Jesus often spoke about. Prayer has a linking and attracting quality in the realm of the invisible. It also has an invigorating and multiplying quality.

Prayer should never be used to influence others, but it can be used to reach the hearts of others and establish therein a state of harmony which often results in happy circumstances. It should be borne in mind, that the greater miracle is that of "God-with-Man" and that our part is to unite with this Divine indwelling, ever seeking ways to banish thoughts that are not in keeping with the God power. Then, much that we achieved would be miraculous, yet all the while seeming to be usual and everyday routine. Such miracles as these are produced by God's power working through us, and this is the kind of miracle we should expect in our lives. When human means fail or when there is an emergency the *other kind* of miracle is needed. It would not do for instance to attempt to live by miracles or our daily life in the physical universe might come to an end.

Prayer is a visualizing, an actually seeing, in the mind's eye, of something that is desired. Many people become too tense about prayer and visualization. They take it too literally and try to see with the inner eyes in exactly the same way as they see with the outer. The more they try to do this, the more the picture recedes. The correct way is to relax, think and try to think of, and try to feel or become aware of, that which is desired. Gradually one is visualizing and one can describe in detail and feel or "take hold in Spirit," that which is desired. We do in fact, "believe that we receive." If you have difficulty with prayer or visualization, stop feeling that it is difficult. This will relax you, and you will feel your way to success.

Only by reaching the heart of others, where their highest instincts and motives live, will you ever be able to change anyone. A miracle is a changed consciousness. Looking into this, I find that those who do not believe in miracles or who have very little success in life are those whose nature is cold, indifferent, cynical; they do not really put their hearts into life. What a change takes place when they do!

The divine power invigorates those who pray and those who are prayed for. Some pray for others and think that provided they have faith, it does not matter if the one who is prayed for has faith or not. This is not so. Jesus said, "Believe ye that I am able to do this?" The one who prays must be linked to the one prayed for by faith and both must be linked to the outflow of the Divine Spirit. Be sure that when you pray for something you desire, pray also for a blessing on others who may desire some similar benefit. Open your heart to all in true loving kindness and into the heart will flow the added blessings of Spirit.

The chief cause of tension is fear, and fear springs from a lack of understanding. Once the individual realizes that Spirit is love, has always been and will always be love, then he relaxes. How can he do otherwise? Many people have been cured of incurable disease, overcome worse circumstances and lifted themselves into illumination by understanding this great and glorious fact. "Know ye not that ye are the temple of God, and that the Spirit of God dwelleth in you?" This is *the* Truth of all Truths in this universe. Let your mind dwell on this, and eventually you will come into the understanding of the love of Spirit.

One must have the faith of the mustard seed. The seed of faith must be in action. Have you wondered what Jesus meant when he said that we need faith "as a grain of mustard seed"? It doesn't mean small-ness, for a speck of dust is small, but he meant that faith should be alive. The mustard seed has the po-tentialities of the mustard tree within it—true faith is a living seed that holds within itself the fulfillment of desire; the Spirit of God is within it as in all living things. By faith, one contacts the eternal, unchanging goodness of Spirit.

We bring about things by constantly thinking of them. Imagine then the harm that one can do himself when he lets his mind go back to the past, over and over again moving into the things he dislikes. Life will go on for him multiplying and manifesting the same things again and again and again in his life. A strong positive understanding of truth will change his con-sciousness and all life will change for him.

This indwelling power is spoken of in the Bible as a child. Throughout the scriptures the child is symboli-cally "the planted consciousness of man in spiritual-ity." It is the spiritual idea—the conscious discovery by you that you have this power within you. Your de-termination to use it is the birth of the child.

The story of the ECK Masters dramatizes this truth. For each is like the ancient prophecy. "Unto us a child is born, unto us a son is given: and the gov-ernment shall be upon his shoulder: and his name shall be called Wonderful, Counsellor, The mighty God, The everlasting Father, The Prince of Peace!"

This description fits the modus operandi of the divine power aptly—that the government shall be upon his shoulders. Once you contact this Spirit within and allow It to take over your responsibilities for you, It will direct and govern all your affairs from the great-est to the least, without effort, without mistakes, and without trouble to you. The moment you hand over your self-government, that is, the burden of making a living, of healing your body, or erasing your mistakes, to the Child, the ECK assumes it with joy.

As soon as you open your consciousness to Spirit, to become the channel, miracles begin to come into your life. It will do things absolutely, irrespective of your present conditions for the betterment of yourself and the whole of humanity. It is no way constrained or constricted by your present condition and circumstances. The whole point here is that Spirit can lift you out of the very circumstances which are restraining your life, and set you down in different and better circumstances. It is the miracle of Spirit.

This power will also be your infallible guide to take you through the threshold beyond the borders of heaven. It is never mistaken in what it does. It only needs to be trusted. All ECK Masters have said, "Heaven and earth may pass away, but I will never leave you."

You must never leave a negative word in this air. The positive word or statement must remain with you, bringing all that is good and desirable into visible form. Now according to the Messenger, this child he spoke of has these qualities: Wonderful Counsellor, the Mighty God, the Everlasting Father, and the Prince of Peace. Look at these and contemplate them. Miracles will start happening in your life.

So long as the individual fixes his attention on the superficial, it is impossible for him to make any progress in knowledge. He is denying the principle of growth, which is the root of all life, whether spiritual, intellectual, or material. He does not stop to reflect that all which he sees as the outer side of things can only result from some germinal principle hidden deep in the center of his being.

This is the Law of Spirit expanding in a necessary

order of sequence. The whole universe is the outcome, alike in one great solidarity of Cosmic Being, as in the separate individualities of its smallest organisms. This great principle is the key to the whole riddle of life, regardless of what plane is viewed. Without this key the door from the outer to the inner side of things can never be opened. A man's life is the exact reflection of the particular stage which he has reached in the perception of the divine nature of his own relation to it.

As we approach the full perception of truth, the life-principle about us expands, and the old bonds and limitations, which had no existence in reality, fall away. We enter into a realm of freedom and beauty. You see, life itself is to be realized as a conscious experience of livingness, beyond and without ourselves. There is the inward Spirit we hold to be ultimate truth. It is liberating to realize that the misconstrued sensation of emptiness and dissatisfaction, which often persists within us, is nothing else than divine discontent pressing forward in declaration that the inner side of things brings forth life to what we observe in the outer.

The central principle, which is at the root of all things, is life, Spirit. But not Spirit as we recognize It in all particular forms of manifestation. It is something more indwelling and concentrated than that. It is that unity of the ECK which is unity, simply because It has not yet passed into diversity. Without It there is no common principle to which we can refer the innumerable forms of manifestation which Spirit assumes.

It is the conception of ECK as the sum total of all Its undistributed powers, being as yet none of these in particular, but all of them in a dormant or latent stage—the inactive area! It is that of the center from which growth takes place by expansion in every direction. It is that which is unknowable, not in the sense of unthinkable, but unanalyzable. It is the subject of perception, not of knowledge, and certainly not of the critical faculty which estimates relations between things, because here we have passed beyond any question of relations, and are face-to-face with the Absolute Spirit.

Of course, the "indwelling" of all is Absolute Spirit. It is Spirit not yet differentiated into any specific manner. It is universal Spirit which pervades all things and is at the heart of all appearance. To come into the knowledge of this is to come into the secret of power, is to enter into the secret place of livingness. As the Psalmist sang in the Ninety-first Psalm, "He that dwelleth in the secret place of the most High shall abide under the shadow of the Almighty."

The presence of this undifferentiated Spirit is the ultimate factor to which all thinking must lead us. On whatever plane one seeks, he must seek only the pure essence, pure energy, pure being, which knows Itself and recognizes Itself, but which cannot dissect Itself because It is not built of parts. Knowing the laws and describing their construction we turn from a breakdown of the parts and rebuild our analogy of Its elements into the whole again. Thus, we gain a power of building up that which always must be beyond the reach of those who regard the unknowable as one with the not-being.

Soul represents the manifestation in a somewhat concrete solidarity of that central life-giving energy, which is not itself on any one plane but generates all planes, the plane of the above, beyond and below. It is at the same time a city, a place of habitation and this is because it is the indwelling place of the living ECK.

I have pointed out previously that one function of Spirit is Its responsiveness to desire. Here we have to go back to the law that the sum of the intelligence of Spirit in the lower degrees of manifestation is not equal to the intelligence of the more complex manifestation. The degree of spiritual intelligence is marked by the whole of the organism through which It finds expression. The more highly organized being has a degree of Spirit which is superior to, and consequently capable of exercising control over, all lower or less fully integrated degrees of ECK.

This being true, we can begin to see why Spirit, the indwelling Spirit of all things, is responsive as well as intelligent.

Being intelligent It knows, and Spirit being ultimately present in infinite forms of Its own ordering is in this: It recognizes Itself and knows Itself, and It knows Its own degrees of being in Its various modes below that of human personality. By this It is bound to respond to Itself in that superior degree which constitutes human personality.

We find that if the subordination of the lower degrees of Spirit to the higher is one of the fundamental laws of the creativeness of thought, there is a salutary restraint upon the abuse of that power. This is the law which keeps us from passing across the borders of heaven into that invisible realm where we can find all things to our choosing. It is a law that we can command the powers of the Spirit for our purposes only in proportion as we first realize and obey their generic character. We can utilize electricity for any purpose as long as we do not require it to pass from a lower to a higher potential.

Then, how do we pass through the borders of heaven? Spirit has an inherent generic character with which we must comply if we would employ It for our specific purposes, and this character is summed up in one word, *ethics*. Since ECK is life, hence Its generic tendency must always be lifeward, outflowing, to increase the livingness of each individual. Since It is the whole It can have no particular interests to serve, and therefore Its actions must always be equally for the benefit of all. Just as water or electricity, or any of the physical forces of the universe will not work contrary to their generic character, Spirit will not work contrary to Its universal character.

If we use Spirit we must follow the Law of ECK which is ethics, Its only limitation. If our originating intention is good, we may employ the spiritual power for what purpose we will. Ethics can be defined as that which is not selfish, which is good for the whole, which will not harm one and will do justice for all concerned—actions for the benefit of all. If we conform to this principle of obedience to the universal, the cosmic Law of spirit, all will be well for ourselves and all others concerned.

We must never lose sight of the old saying that "a truth on one plane is a truth on all." If a principle exists at all, it exists universally. We must not allow ourselves to be misled by appearances, remembering that the perceptible results of the working of any principle consists of two factors: The principle itself, and the application of the principle. The former is invariable, and the latter is variable. The operation of the same invariable upon different variables must necessarily produce a variety of results.

Needless to say, the generation of power by attraction applies to the spiritual as well as to the physical plane. It acts with the same mathematical precision on both planes. The human individuality consists not in the mere aggregation of its parts, whether spiritual or material but in the unity of power resulting from intimate association as parts enter with one another. This, according to the principle of the generating of power by attraction, is infinitely superior both in intelligence and power, to any less fully integrated mode of Spirit. This accounts for all claims that have ever been made for the creative power of our thought being superior over all things that come within the circle of our own particular life. Thus, it is, that each man is the center of his universe, and has the power, by directing his own thought, to control all things.

Each man, as the center of his own universe, is himself centered in a higher system in which he is only one of innumerable similar atoms, and this system again is in a higher plane until we reach the supreme center of all things. For the reason that Spirit is expansive, and does expand from the individual, then he, in time, can embrace the whole universe, and perhaps all planes of cosmic existence.

Nevertheless, when we look to the infinity of Spirit, of which our individuality is a singular expression, we do so because in looking upward we are looking for the higher degrees of ourself. The reason being, that Spirit must respond to the individual consciousness in obedience to our wishes, and manifest as Its own individuality, and as a necessary inflow of intelligence and power.

By the inflow of Its power, Spirit furnishes the basis of freedom, charity, and wisdom, as a whole and not in parts, as it does not work in that fashion. Thus, by a natural law the demand creates the supply and this supply may be freely applied to any and every subject matter that entrusts itself to it. There is no limit to this supply of energy other than what we ourselves possess by thought. Nor is there any limit to the purposes we make it serve other than the one law of order, which says that it must be used for the benefit of all on an ethical level.

When we have learned and grasped what is said here, there is little need for anyone to stay on the threshold of heaven. By depending on Divine Spirit, by depending on the whole and by trusting It we can enter into the realm of the unseen of the higher consciousness.

Spirit has three main qualities, which are: Freedom, Charity, and Wisdom. It is a general force working through specializing agents or consciousness upon the plane of the particular. It is a forming power that works in a creative way. It has the power to react upon Itself when there are no conscious agents through which It can operate. On every plane, Life Force, or Spirit, operates in a similar manner to that of this plane, though at a higher creative level. It penetrates all planes, all life-forms, which are the effect of this power. Divine ECK works at Its best when Its distributing agent, the Soul, uses Its higher qualities of freedom, charity, and wisdom. These, united with the individual consciousness as wavelengths of a specializing nature through Soul, create effects upon the planes and the life-forms existing there.

In conclusion, I mention here that if you do not grasp the principles as laid down here, reread the major points in this book often, until you have them integrated into your consciousness. The unfoldment of truth will be revealed in hundreds of material and spiritual aspects on all planes and you may leave your body at your own time, and by your own will, to travel through the worlds beyond.

Glossary

Words set in SMALL CAPS are defined elsewhere in this glossary.

CHELA. *CHEE-lah* A spiritual student.

ECK. *EHK* The Life Force, the Holy Spirit, or Audible Life Current which sustains all life.

ECKANKAR. *EHK-ahn-kahr* Religion of the Light and Sound of God. Also known as the Ancient Science of SOUL TRAVEL. A truly spiritual religion for the individual in modern times. The teachings provide a framework for anyone to explore their own spiritual experiences. Established by PAUL TWITCHELL, the modern-day founder, in 1965. The word means "Co-worker with God."

ECK MASTERS. Spiritual Masters who can assist and protect people in their spiritual studies and travels. The ECK Masters are from a long line of God-Realized SOULS who know the responsibility that goes with spiritual freedom.

GOD-REALIZATION. The state of God Consciousness. Complete and conscious awareness of God.

HU. *HYOO* The most ancient, secret name for God. The singing of the word *HU* is considered a love song to God. It can be sung aloud or silently to oneself.

INITIATION. Earned by a member of ECKANKAR through spiritual unfoldment and service to God. The initiation is a private ceremony in which the individual is linked to the Sound and Light of God.

KLEMP, HAROLD. The present MAHANTA, the LIVING ECK MASTER. SRI HAROLD KLEMP became the MAHANTA, the LIVING ECK MASTER

197

in 1981. The spiritual name of Sri Harold Klemp is WAH Z.

LAI TSI. *lie TSEE* An ancient Chinese ECK MASTER.

LIVING ECK MASTER. The title of the spiritual leader of
ECKANKAR. His duty is to lead SOUL back to God. The Living ECK
Master can assist spiritual students physically as the Outer
Master, in the dream state as the Dream Master, and in the
spiritual worlds as the Inner Master.

MAHANTA. *mah-HAHN-tah* A title to describe the highest state
of God Consciousness on earth, often embodied in the LIVING
ECK MASTER. He is the Living Word. An expression of the Spirit
of God that is always with you.

PLANES. The levels of existence, such as the Physical, Astral,
Causal, Mental, Etheric, and SOUL Planes.

REBAZAR TARZS. *REE-bah-zahr TAHRZ* A Tibetan ECK MASTER
known as the torchbearer of ECKANKAR in the lower worlds.

SELF-REALIZATION. SOUL recognition. The entering of Soul into the
Soul Plane and there beholding Itself as pure Spirit. A state of
seeing, knowing, and being.

THE SHARIYAT-KI-SUGMAD. *SHAH-ree-aht-kee-SOOG-mahd* The
sacred scriptures of ECKANKAR. The scriptures are comprised of
about twelve volumes in the spiritual worlds. The first two were
transcribed from the inner PLANES by PAUL TWITCHELL, modern-
day founder of ECKANKAR.

SOUL. The True Self. The inner, most sacred part of each person.
Soul exists before birth and lives on after the death of the
physical body. As a spark of God, Soul can see, know, and
perceive all things. It is the creative center of Its own world.

SOUL TRAVEL. The expansion of consciousness. The ability of SOUL
to transcend the physical body and travel into the spiritual
worlds of God. Soul Travel is taught only by the LIVING ECK
MASTER. It helps people unfold spiritually and can provide proof
of the existence of God and life after death.

SOUND AND LIGHT OF ECK. The Holy Spirit. The two aspects
through which God appears in the lower worlds. People can
experience them by looking and listening within themselves
and through SOUL TRAVEL.

SPIRITUAL EXERCISES OF ECK. The daily practice of certain techniques to get us in touch with the Light and Sound of God.

SRI. *SREE* A title of spiritual respect, similar to reverend or pastor, used for those who have attained the Kingdom of God. In ECKANKAR, it is reserved for the MAHANTA, the LIVING ECK MASTER.

SUGMAD. *SOOG-mahd* A sacred name for God. Sugmad is neither masculine nor feminine; It is the source of all life.

TWITCHELL, PAUL. An American ECK MASTER who brought the modern teachings of ECKANKAR to the world through his writings and lectures.

VAIRAG. *vie-RAHG* Detachment.

WAH Z. *WAH zee* The spiritual name of SRI HAROLD KLEMP. It means the Secret Doctrine. It is his name in the spiritual worlds.

For more explanations of ECKANKAR terms, see *A Cosmic Sea of Words: The ECKANKAR Lexicon* by Harold Klemp.

Index

201

Index

Index

Index

For Further Reading and Study

Past Lives, Dreams, and Soul Travel
Harold Klemp

What if you could recall past-life lessons for advantage today? What if you could learn the secret knowledge of dreams to gain the wisdom of the heart? Or Soul Travel, to master the shift in consciousness needed to find peace and contentment? To ride the waves of God's love and mercy? Let Harold Klemp, leading authority in all three fields, show you how.

This book can help you find your true purpose, greater love than you've ever known, and spiritual freedom.

How to Survive Spiritually in Our Times,
Mahanta Transcripts, Book 16
Harold Klemp

A master storyteller, Harold Klemp weaves stories, tips, and techniques into the golden fabric of his talks. They highlight the deeper truths within you, so you can apply them in your life *now*. He speaks right to Soul. It is that divine, eternal spark that you are. The survivor. Yet survival is only the starting point in your spiritual life. Harold Klemp also shows you how to gain in spiritual wealth. This book's a treasure.

Autobiography of a Modern Prophet
Harold Klemp

Master your true destiny. Learn how this man's journey to God illuminates the way for you too. Dare to explore the outer limits of the last great frontier, your spiritual worlds! The more you explore them, the sooner you come to discovering your true nature as an infinite, eternal spark of God. This book helps you get there! A good read.

Stranger by the River
Paul Twitchell

A poetic dialogue between the ECK Master Rebazar Tarzs and the Seeker. Through their conversation, you'll learn about the nature of God, love, wisdom, freedom, purity, and death. Its classic style is reminiscent of Kahil Gibran's *The Prophet*.

Available at your local bookstore. If unavailable, call (952) 380-2222. Or write: ECKANKAR, Dept. BK8, P.O. Box 27300, Minneapolis, MN 55427 U.S.A.

There May Be an Eckankar Study Group near You

Eckankar offers a variety of local and international activities for the spiritual seeker. With hundreds of study groups worldwide, Eckankar is near you! Many areas have Eckankar centers where you can browse through the books in a quiet, unpressured environment, talk with others who share an interest in this ancient teaching, and attend beginning discussion classes on how to gain the attributes of Soul: wisdom, power, love, and freedom.

Around the world, Eckankar study groups offer special one-day or weekend seminars on the basic teachings of Eckankar. For membership information, visit the Eckankar Web site (www.eckankar.org). For the location of the Eckankar center or study group nearest you, click on "Other Eckankar Web sites" for a listing of those areas with Web sites. You're also welcome to check your phone book under **ECKANKAR**; call **(952) 380-2222, Ext. BK8;** or write **ECKANKAR, Att: Information, BK8, P.O. Box 27300, Minneapolis, MN 55427 U.S.A.**

☐ Please send me information on the nearest Eckankar center or study group in my area.

☐ Please send me more information about membership in Eckankar, which includes a twelve-month spiritual study.

Please type or print clearly

Name _____
         first (given)   last (family)

Street _____ Apt. # _____

City _____ State/Prov. _____

Zip/Postal Code _____ Country _____

213

About the Author

Paul Twitchell made Eckankar known to the modern world in 1965. He separated spiritual truths from the cultural trappings which had surrounded them. Everyday people could begin to experience the Light and Sound of God while living happy, steady, and productive lives.

Born in Kentucky in the early part of the twentieth century, Paul Twitchell served in the U.S. Navy during the Second World War.

A seeker from an early age, he was introduced to a group of spiritual Masters who would change the course of his life. These were the Vairagi ECK Masters. While they trained Paul to become the Living ECK Master, he explored a wide range of spiritual traditions under many teachers. The high teachings of ECK had been scattered to the four corners of the world. Paul gathered these golden teachings of Light and Sound and made them readily available to us.

It was these God experiences he chronicled in his book *The Tiger's Fang*. Paul Twitchell eventually joined the Vairagi Order and was given the task of bringing Eckankar to the world. He became the Living ECK Master.

By 1965, Paul was conducting Soul Travel workshops in California and Eckankar began to grow. Paul ll died in 1971, after he initiated many into the eachings.

ne present Living ECK Master is Sri Harold Klemp. He continues in Paul Twitchell's footsteps, giving new life to the age-old spiritual teachings of ECK.